DATE DUE			
Apr 11 '83			
GAYLORD M-2			PRINTED IN U.S.A.

Fugitive Bibliographies

Thomas Daniel Young, GENERAL EDITOR

∴

ROBERT PENN WARREN

Robert Penn Warren

A BIBLIOGRAPHY

COMPILED BY

Mary Nance Huff

NEW YORK, *David Lewis*

1968

Printed in the United States of America.
Library of Congress Catalog Card Number: 68-28007

FIRST PRINTING

Manufactured by Haddon Craftsmen, Inc.
DESIGNED BY HERBERT JOHNSON

Robert Penn Warren

Many critics and literary historians argue that the South has dominated the American literary scene for much of the twentieth century. To support this contention they cite the lengthy list of Southerners who during the past thirty or forty years have made significant contributions to American letters: William Faulkner, Ellen Glasgow, Thomas Wolfe, Katherine Anne Porter, Elizabeth Madox Roberts, Eudora Welty, Flannery O'Connor, James Branch Cabell, Richard Wright, Tennessee Williams, Caroline Gordon, Andrew Nelson Lytle, John Gould Fletcher, and Stark Young. And this list, though not intended to be exhaustive, is obviously deficient because it does not include the names of the Fugitive group—John Crowe Ransom, Allen Tate, Donald Davidson, and Robert Penn Warren. Among the most articulate literary men America has produced, these four have published almost a hundred volumes, and Louise Cowan credits them with being the inaugurators of this Southern literary renaissance:

> In poetry, in fiction, and in literary criticism, these men have taken their place among the most noted writers today in English. Their greatest impact, however, has been in establishing a profession of letters, as much by their work in editing and setting policies for literary journals as by transforming the study of literature in the universities, their texts and their own teaching demonstrating the necessity of its being approached as an important study in its own right. Genuine men of letters, in that they pursue their crafts on many fronts at once and in that they allow their critical ideas to interact with their creative imaginations, they are a group unmatched in American literature.
>
> (*The Fugitive Group: A Literary History*, p. xix.)

The most versatile of this distinguished group, Robert Penn Warren has made significant contributions to almost every literary genre: biography, fiction, drama, poetry, and criticism. He is the only writer who has ever received the Pulitzer Prize for both fiction (*All the King's Men*, 1946) and poetry (*Promises*, 1957).

Best known, perhaps, for his fiction, Warren's eight novels and many of his short stories probe deeply and broadly into the American past, from the frontier (*World Enough and Time*) through the Civil War and Reconstruction (*Wilderness* and *Band of Angels*) to some of the most crucial times of the twentieth century: the early 1900's (*Night Rider*), the twenties (*At Heaven's Gate*), the thirties (*All the King's Men*) and the fifties (*Flood*). In addition to his interest in the past, Warren shares other feelings and convictions with such Southern contemporaries as Andrew Lytle, Allen Tate, and William Faulkner: the importance of the family, the sense of a continuous tradition, and the superiority of an agrarian society. Although his novels depict vividly a particular time and place—and develop conflicts resulting from situations based partly on historical fact—they are not propagandistic. Their major concern is with the constant and universal in human behavior, with the problems which have tormented man in the past and will continue to plague him in the future. His characters constantly struggle to live a life of honor, to maintain a feeling of self-respect, in the face of an always complex and often hostile world. The artist's social responsibility, Warren has written, is to create the myth that will "render his total vision of the world, his sense of individual destiny, his sense of man's place in nature, and his sense of history and society." (*Selected Essays*, p. 48.)

The popular success of some of the fiction has made many readers unaware that Warren is a genuinely gifted poet. Equally prolific in both forms, for more than forty years he has produced a steady flow of verse. (His first poem *Crusade* was printed in *The Fugitive* for June, 1923.) His initial volume of poetry, *Thirty-Six Poems* (1935) has been followed by six others: *Eleven Poems on the Same Theme* (1942); *Selected Poems, 1923-1943* (1944); *Brother to Dragons* (1953); *Promises: Poems 1954-1956* (1957); *You, Emperors, and Others: Poems 1957-1960* (1960); and *Selected Poems: New and Old 1923-1966* (1967).

Warren's poetry, as John M. Bradbury has written of "Original Sin: A Short Story," reads like a "tightly condensed version of a Warren novel." Like the novels, too, the poems, though firmly rooted in the lore and traditions of the South, show the artist's deep concern for the elemental and universal facts of human existence. In an essay on Robert Frost, Warren defines the poet as one who is "greatly concerned with the flux of things, with the texture of the world, with, even, the dark 'natural' places of man's soul." This definition is an adequate statement of Warren's intentions in much of his poetry. Poem after poem follows what Warren has called, "the main line of my impulse": the flow of time, the influence of the past on the present, and the necessity for self-knowledge. The speaker in the poems, as he contemplates his personal past and "the past that lies behind that past," often tries to escape the realization of his own depravity only to discover that he is brother to dragons. Rich in texture and remarkably varied in structure and metrical form, Warren's best poems can stand comparison with any poetry, except the very greatest, produced in this century.

Despite the brilliance of his productions in these areas, however, Warren's contributions to modern letters cannot be assessed by an evaluation of his fiction and poetry. His *John Brown: The Making of a Martyr* (1929) is a first-rate biography. And he is one of the most important critics of his generation. If one seeks the most perceptive and illuminating discussion of a contemporary author—as, for example, William Faulkner, Eudora Welty, John Crowe Ransom, Katherine Anne Porter, or Peter Taylor—he will often find what he wants in an essay by Robert Penn Warren. From 1935 to 1942 Warren, along with Cleanth Brooks and Charles Pipkin, edited the *Southern Review*. One of the most distinguished literary quarterlies ever published in America, the *Review* carried important essays, stories, and poems by such established writers as Herbert Agar, Kenneth Burke, T. S. Eliot, John Crowe Ransom, Donald Davidson, Wallace Stevens, Katherine Anne Porter, and Allen Tate. It was also one of the first journals to publish such important newcomers as R. P. Blackmur, Randall Jarrell, F. O. Matthiessen, Mary McCarthy, and Eudora Welty. Warren's association with Cleanth Brooks also produced two of the most influential textbooks of the century, *Understanding Poetry* (1938) and *Understanding Fiction* (1943). To say that these two books have revolutionized the way literature is taught to undergraduates is hardly an overstatement. In addition to his fiction, poetry, criticism, editing, and textbooks, Warren is a highly respected teacher and a competent journalist. His *Legacy of the Civil War* and his two studies of segregation give valuable insights into some of the most critical and controversial political and social issues of our time. No other writer in this century has attempted so many literary forms and produced work of such consistently high quality in all of them.

2

In spite of Warren's distinguished career as man of letters, no one has collected the pertinent information concerning Warren's own writing and the most significant of the commentary about him. This bibliography, which proposes to fill this need, has relied heavily upon the brief checklists that appear in the following works:

Leonard Casper, *Robert Penn Warren: The Dark and Bloody Ground*, (Seattle: University of Washington Press, 1960).
Charles H. Bohner, *Robert Penn Warren* (New York: Twayne Publishers, Inc., 1964).
Paul West, *Robert Penn Warren* (University of Minnesota Pamphlets on American Writers, No. 44, 1964).
John Lewis Longley, Jr., *Robert Penn Warren: A Collection of Critical Essays* (New York: New York University Press, 1965).
John M. Bradbury, *The Fugitives: A Critical Account* (Chapel Hill: University of North Carolina Press, 1958).

The following checklists, although highly selective, have also been most helpful: Robert Wooster Stallman's in the *University of Kansas City Review*, XIV (Autumn, 1947), 78-83; Frederick P. W. McDowell's in *Accent*, XV (Summer, 1955), 173-196; Maurice Beebe and Erin Marcus's in *Modern Fiction Studies*, VI

(Spring, 1960), 83-88; and the bibliographical supplement to the *Literary History of the United States*, pp. 234-36.

This bibliography is divided into eight sections:

I. Books, arranged chronologically according to the original date of publication.

II. Translations of Warren's books, arranged alphabetically according to the English title of each book translated; the entries under each English title are listed chronologically.

III. Short stories, arranged alphabetically according to title.

IV. Poems, arranged alphabetically according to title.

V. Essays and articles, arranged alphabetically according to title.

VI. Book reviews, arranged alphabetically by the last name of the author of the book reviewed.

VII. Miscellanea, arranged alphabetically according to title.

VIII. Biographical and critical material, arranged alphabetically according to the name of the author, with brief descriptive annotation.

In Section One the individual listings are subdivided; the table of contents of each book is followed by a selective list of significant reviews, both signed and unsigned. Signed reviews are given first, alphabetically by reviewer's surname; unsigned reviews are listed alphabetically by name of the publication in which the review appeared. The listings of poems and stories give first information concerning their initial publication followed by a chronological list of all subsequent publications in Warren's own collections. The same procedure is followed with the essays and articles except that their publication record is given for major anthologies as well as in Warren's own collections.

This bibliography attempts to include all work by Warren and the most significant about him through 1967. Material primarily concerned with the Fugitives, the Agrarians, or the New Criticism has not been included. Although every reasonable effort has been made in an attempt to insure the completeness and accuracy of this bibliography, inaccuracies and omissions are almost certain to occur. In an attempt to keep such errors to a minimum, almost every item listed has been examined by the editors. The few exceptions are indicated by an asterisk.

Anyone who has attempted to compile a bibliography knows the extent of our indebtedness to many libraries and librarians. Particularly we wish to express our gratitude to the staffs of The Joint Universities Library, Nashville, and The Library of Congress.

MARY NANCE HUFF
THOMAS DANIEL YOUNG

Nashville, Tennessee
March 1, 1968

Contents

Robert Penn Warren

A BIBLIOGRAPHY

I. Books

John Brown: The Making of a Martyr. (Biography.) New York: Payson & Clarke Ltd., 1929.

Signed Reviews

Craven, Avery. *New York Herald Tribune Books,* VI (January 12, 1930), 17.

Ehrlich, Leonard. *New York Evening Post,* November 16, 1929, p. 13m.

Gabriel, R. H. *Yale Review,* XIX (Spring, 1930), 595.

Kelly, F. F. *New York Times Book Review,* January 12, 1930, p. 7.

MacDonald, William. *Nation,* CXXXI (July 2, 1930), 22-23.

Munson, G. B. *Bookman,* LXXI (March, 1930), 114.

Nevins, Allan. *New Republic,* LXII (March 19, 1930), 134-135.

Perkins, Dexter. *Virginia Quarterly Review,* VI (October, 1930), 615-618.

Robbins, Frances Lamont. *Outlook and Independent,* CLIII (November 13, 1929), 427.

Sifton, Paul. *The World* [New York], December 1, 1929, p. 11m.

Snow, Francis. *Current History,* XXXI (February, 1930), 836.

Unsigned Reviews

* *Cleveland Open Shelf,* February, 1930, p. 28.

Historical Outlook, XXI (April, 1930), 186.

Springfield [Massachusetts] *Sunday Union and Republican,* January 12, 1930, p. 7e.

John Brown: The Making of a Martyr. New York: Harcourt, Brace & Company, Inc., 1929. (Reissue.)

Thirty-Six Poems. (Poems.) New York: The Alcestis Press, 1935.

Contents

"The Return: An Elegy"
"Kentucky Mountain Farm"
i. "Rebuke of the Rocks"
ii. "At the Hour of the Breaking of the Rocks"
iii. "History among the Rocks"
iv. "The Cardinal"
v. "The Jay"
vi. "Watershed"
vii. "The Return"
"Pondy Woods"
"Eidolon"
"Letter of a Mother"
"Genealogy"
"History"
"Resolution"
"Letter from a Coward to a Hero"
"Late Subterfuge"
"Ransom"
"Aged Man Surveys the Past Time"
"Toward Rationality"
"To a Friend Parting"
"Letter to a Friend"
"Aubade for Hope"
"Man Coming of Age"
"Croesus in Autumn"
"So Frost Astounds"
"The Last Metaphor"
"Pacific Gazer"
"Calendar"
"Problem of Knowledge"
"Cold Colloquy"
"For a Self-possessed Friend"
"For a Friend Who Thinks Himself Urbane"

"The Garden"
"To One Awake"
"Garden Waters"
"To a Face in the Crowd"

Signed Reviews

Flint, F. Cudworth. *Southern Review,* I (Winter, 1936), 672-674.

Holmes, John. *Virginia Quarterly Review,* XII (April, 1936), 292, 294-295.

Lann, Robert. *New Republic,* LXXXVII (July 15, 1936), 304.

Leach, H. G. *Forum,* XCVI (August, 1936), 96.

Lechlitner, Ruth. *New York Herald Tribune Books,* February 16, 1936, p. 10.

Zabel, M. D. *Poetry,* XLVIII (April, 1936), 37-41.

Unsigned Review

Nation, CXLII (March 25, 1936), 391.

An Approach to Literature: A Collection of Prose and Verse with Analyses and Discussions. By Cleanth Brooks, Jr., John Thibaut Purser, and Robert Penn Warren. (Textbook.) Baton Rouge: Louisiana State University Press, 1936.

An Approach to Literature: A Collection of Prose and Verse, with Analyses and Discussions. By Cleanth Brooks, Jr., John Thibaut Purser, and Robert Penn Warren. Revised edition. New York: F. S. Crofts & Co., 1939.

An Approach to Literature. By Cleanth Brooks, John Thibaut Purser, and Robert Penn Warren. Third edition. New York: Appleton-Century-Crofts, 1952.

An Approach to Literature. By Cleanth Brooks, John Thibaut Purser, and Robert Penn Warren. Fourth edition. New York: Appleton-Century-Crofts, 1964.

A Southern Harvest: Short Stories by Southern Writers. Edited by Robert Penn Warren. (Short stories.) Boston: Houghton Mifflin Company, 1937.

Signed Reviews

Armfield, Eugene. *Saturday Review of Literature*, XVII (December 18, 1937), 10-11.

Clark, Eleanor. *Partisan Review*, IV (March, 1938), 56-58.

W., M. *New York Times Book Review*, November 21, 1937, p. 28.

Unsigned Review

New York Herald Tribune Books, XIV (January 9, 1938), 17.

A Southern Harvest: Short Stories by Southern Writers. Edited by Robert Penn Warren. Toronto: Thomas Allen, 1937. (Reissue.)

Understanding Poetry: An Anthology for College Students. By Cleanth Brooks, Jr., and Robert Penn Warren. (Textbook.) New York: Henry Holt and Company, 1938.

Signed Reviews

Holmes, John. *Boston Evening Transcript*, August 6, 1938, sec. 3, p. 2.

Koch, Vivienne C. *Quarterly Journal of Speech*, XXV (October, 1939), 499-500.

Walton, E. L. *New York Herald Tribune Books*, XIV (August 28, 1938), 17.

Understanding Poetry: An Anthology for College Students. By Cleanth Brooks and Robert Penn Warren. Revised complete edition. New York: Holt, 1950.

Signed Review

Kenner, Hugh. *Poetry*, LXXXIV (April, 1954), 45-48.

Understanding Poetry: An Anthology for College Students. By Cleanth Brooks and Robert Penn Warren. Revised shorter edition. New York: Holt, 1950.

Understanding Poetry: An Anthology for College Students. By Cleanth Brooks and Robert Penn Warren. Revised complete edition. New York: Holt, 1956.

Understanding Poetry. By Cleanth Brooks and Robert Penn Warren. Third edition. New York: Holt, Rinehart and Winston, 1960.

Night Rider. (Novel.) Boston: Houghton Mifflin Company, 1939.

Signed Reviews

Baker, Howard. *Southern Review*, V (Spring, 1940), 793.
Curtiss, Mina. *Nation*, CXLVIII (April 29, 1939), 507-508.
Davenport, Basil. *Saturday Review of Literature*, XIX (March 18, 1939), 6.
Davis, Hassoldt. *New York Times Book Review*, XLIV (March 19, 1939), 6.
Fadiman, Clifton. *New Yorker*, XV (March 18, 1939), 68-69.
Isherwood, Christopher. *New Republic*, LXXXXIX [*sic*] (May 31, 1939), 108.
Muller, Herbert J. *Kenyon Review*, I (Summer, 1939), 323-324.
Pruette, Lorine. *New York Herald Tribune Books*, XV (March 19, 1939), 2.
Rahv, Philip. *Partisan Review*, VI (Spring, 1939), 112-113.
Stegner, Wallace. *Virginia Quarterly Review*, XV (Summer, 1939), 443-444.
T., F. H. *Vanderbilt Alumnus*, XXIV (April, 1939), 10-11.
Thompson, Ralph. *Yale Review*, XXVIII (June, 1939), vi.
Woodward, Frances. *Atlantic Monthly*, CLXIII (April, 1939), [page unnumbered]. (In "The Atlantic Bookshelf" supplement to *The Atlantic Monthly*.)

Unsigned Reviews

Booklist, XXXV (April 15, 1939), 271.
Springfield [Massachusetts] *Sunday Union and Republican*, April 9, 1939, p. 7e.
Time, XXXIII (March 27, 1939), 73.

Night Rider. Toronto: Thomas Allen, 1939. (Reissue.)

Night Rider. London: Eyre & Spottiswoode Ltd., 1940. (Reissue.)

Signed Review

West, Anthony. *New Statesman and Nation,* XIX (January 20, 1940), 77.

Unsigned Review

[London] *Times Literary Supplement,* January 20, 1940, p. 29.

Night Rider. New York: Random House, Inc., 1948. (Reissue.)

Night Rider. Abridgment and introduction by George Mayberry. New York: New American Library, 1950. (A Signet book, No. 804.)

Night Rider. London: Eyre & Spottiswoode Ltd., 1955. (Reissue.)

Signed Review

Wilson, Angus. *Encounter,* IV (May, 1955), 75-78.

Night Rider. New York: Berkley Publishing Corp., 1956. (Reissue.)

Night Rider. New York: Random House, Inc., 1958. (Reissue.)

Night Rider. London: Landsborough Publications, 1959. (Reissue.)

Eleven Poems on the Same Theme. (Poems.) Norfolk, Conn.: New Directions, 1942.

Contents

"Monologue at Midnight"
"Bearded Oaks"
"Picnic Remembered"
"Crime'
"Original Sin: A Short Story"
"End of Season"
"Revelation"
"Pursuit"
"Question and Answer"
"Love's Parable"
"Terror"

Signed Reviews

Deutsch, Babette. *New Republic*, CVIII (March 29, 1943), 420.

Jack, Peter Monro. *New York Times Book Review*, April 26, 1942, p. 4.

Jones, Frank. *Nation*, CLV (September 26, 1942), 277.

Lechlitner, Ruth. *New York Herald Tribune Books*, July 19, 1942, p. 13.

Nims, John Frederick. *Poetry*, LXI (December, 1942), 505-508.

Rushton, Peters. *Virginia Quarterly Review*, XVIII (Summer, 1942), 479-480.

Untermeyer, Louis. *Yale Review*, XXXII (Winter, 1943), 370.

Williams, Oscar. *New Republic*, CVII (July 6, 1942), 28.

Unsigned Review

New Yorker, XVIII (May 9, 1942), 80.

At Heaven's Gate. (Novel.) New York: Harcourt, Brace and Company, 1943.

Signed Reviews

Cowley, Malcolm. *New Republic*, CIX (August 23, 1943), 258.

Daniels, Jonathan. *Saturday Review of Literature*, XXVI (August 21, 1943), 6.

Garrigue, Jean. *Kenyon Review*, VI (Winter, 1944), 135-138.

Geismar, Maxwell. *New York Times Book Review*, August 22, 1943, p. 4.

Gordon, Caroline. *New York Herald Tribune Weekly Book Review*, XIX (August 22, 1943), 5.

Kelley, H. G. *Library Journal*, LXVIII (August, 1943), 625.

Laughlin, James. *Accent*, IV (Autumn, 1943), 62-63.

North, Sterling. *Chicago Sun Book Week*, I (August 22, 1943), 3.

Phillips, William. *Nation*, CLVII (August 28, 1943), 243-244.

Prescott, Orville. *Yale Review*, XXXIII (Autumn, 1943), xii.

Stevenson, Lionel. *Virginia Quarterly Review*, XX (Winter, 1944), 144-145.

Varley, Lee. *Springfield* [Massachusetts] *Sunday Union and Republican*, August 1, 1943, p. 7e.

Unsigned Reviews

Atlantic Monthly, CLXXII (September, 1943), 131.
Christian Century, LX (September 1, 1943), 991.
Commonweal, XXXVIII (August 6, 1943), 398.
New Yorker, XIX (August 21, 1943), 67.

At Heaven's Gate. London: Eyre & Spottiswoode Ltd., 1943. (Reissue.)

At Heaven's Gate. Toronto: George J. McLeod, Ltd., 1943. (Reissue.)

At Heaven's Gate. Abridgment and introduction by George Mayberry. A special edition. New York: New American Library, 1949. (A Signet book, No. 725.)

At Heaven's Gate. New York: Random House, 1959. (Reissue.)

At Heaven's Gate. London: Eyre & Spottiswoode Ltd., 1960. (Reissue.)

Signed Reviews

Jacobson, Dan. *Spectator*, CCIV (January 15, 1960), 83.

Price, R. G. G. *Punch*, CCXXXVIII (January 20, 1960), 139.

Waterhouse, Keith. *New Statesman*, LIX (January 16, 1960), 79.

Unsigned Review

[London] *Times Literary Supplement*, January 15, 1960, p. 29.

At Heaven's Gate. New York: New American Library, 1963. (A Signet book, No. T2298.)

Understanding Fiction. By Cleanth Brooks, Jr., and Robert Penn Warren. (Textbook.) New York: F. S. Crofts & Company, 1943.

Signed Review

Hintz, H. W. *College English*, V (October, 1943), 48.

Understanding Fiction. By Cleanth Brooks and Robert Penn Warren. Second edition. New York: Appleton-Century-Crofts, 1959.

Selected Poems, 1923-1943. (Poems.) New York: Harcourt, Brace and Company, 1944.

Contents

"The Ballad of Billie Potts"
"Terror"
"Pursuit"
"Original Sin: A Short Story"
"Crime"
"Letter from a Coward to a Hero"
"History"
"Question and Answer"
"End of Season"
"Ransom"
"Aged Man Surveys the Past Time"
"Toward Rationality"
"To a Friend Parting"
"Letter to a Friend"
"Aubade for Hope"
"Eidolon"
"Revelation"
"Variation: Ode to Fear"
"Mexico Is a Foreign Country: Five Studies in Naturalism"
I. "Butterflies over the Map"
II. "Siesta Time in Village Plaza by Ruined Bandstand and Banana Tree"

III. "The World Comes Galloping: A True Story"
IV. "Small Soldiers with Drum in Large Landscape"
V. "The Mango on the Mango Tree"
"Monologue at Midnight"
"Bearded Oaks"
"Picnic Remembered"
"Resolution"
"Love's Parable"
"Late Subterfuge"
"Man Coming of Age"
"The Garden"
"The Return: An Elegy"
"Kentucky Mountain Farm"
I. "Rebuke of the Rocks"
II. "At the Hour of the Breaking of the Rocks"
III. "History Among the Rocks"
IV. "The Cardinal"
V. "The Jay"
VI. "Watershed"
VII. "The Return"
"Pondy Woods"
"Letter of a Mother"
"Croesus in Autumn"
"So Frost Astounds"
"The Last Metaphor"
"Pacific Gazer"
"Calendar"
"Problem of Knowledge"
"For a Self-possessed Friend"
"For a Friend Who Thinks Himself Urbane"
"Cold Colloquy"
"Garden Waters"
"To a Face in a Crowd"

Signed Reviews

Arrowsmith, William. *Chimera*, II (Summer, 1944), 44-45.
Bogan, Louise. *New Yorker*, XX (April 22, 1944), 85.

Drew, Elizabeth. *New York Herald Tribune Weekly Book Review*, XX (June 25, 1944), 11.

Dupee, F. W. *Nation*, CLIX (November 25, 1944), 660, 662.

Fitts, Dudley. *Poetry*, LXV (November, 1944), 94-101.

Gregory, Horace. *Sewanee Review*, LII (Autumn, 1944), 575-578, 587.

Herschberger, Ruth. *Accent*, IV (Summer, 1944), 240-246.

Kennedy, Leo. *The Chicago Sun Book Week*, I (April 16, 1944), 6.

Matthiessen, F. O. *Kenyon Review*, VI (Autumn, 1944), 690-693.

Mizener, Arthur. *Partisan Review*, XI (Summer, 1944), 359-360.

Ransom, John Crowe. *Saturday Review of Literature*, XXVII (May 20, 1944), 10-11.

Thorp, Willard. *New York Times Book Review*, XLIX (May 7, 1944), 4.

Untermeyer, Louis. *Yale Review*, XXXIV (Winter, 1945), 344.

Van Ghent, Dorothy. *Rocky Mountain Review*, VIII (Summer, 1944), 164-165.

Selected Poems, 1923-1943. Toronto: George J. McLeod, Ltd., 1944. (Reissue.)

Selected Poems, 1923-1943. London: Fortune Press, Ltd., 1951. (Reissue.)

All the King's Men. (Novel.) New York: Harcourt, Brace and Company, 1946.

Signed Reviews

Davis, Robert Gorham. *New York Times Book Review*, LI (August 18, 1946), 3, 24.

Dexter, Ethel Hathaway. *Springfield* [Massachusetts] *Sunday Union and Republican*, September 1, 1946, p. 4d.

Fergusson, Francis. *Perspectives USA*, No. 6 (Winter, 1954), 30-44.

Hardwick, Elizabeth. *Partisan Review*, XIII (November-December, 1946), 583-584.

Heilman, Robert B. *Sewanee Review*, LV (January-March, 1947), 154-166.

Jackson, Joseph Henry. *This World*, in *San Francisco Chronicle*, August 18, 1946, p. 12.

Marsh, Fred. *New York Herald Tribune Weekly Book Review*, XXII (August 18, 1946), 2.

Mayberry, George. *New Republic*, CXV (September 2, 1946), 265-266.

Prescott, Orville, *Yale Review*, XXXVI (Autumn, 1946), 192.

R., W. K. *Christian Science Monitor*, September 4, 1946, p. [14].

Rago, Henry. *Commonweal*, XLIV (October 4, 1946), 599-600.

Smith, L. C. *The Chicago Sun Book Week*, IV (August 18, 1946), 3.

Trilling, Diana. *Nation*, CLXIII (August 24, 1946), 220.

Wade, John Donald. *Virginia Quarterly Review*, XXIII (Winter, 1947), 138-141.

Walbridge, E. F. *Library Journal*, LXXI (August, 1946), 1051.

Wood, J. P. *Saturday Review of Literature*, XXIX (August 17, 1946), 11.

Unsigned Reviews

Booklist, XLIII (September, 1946), 18.

Catholic World, CLXIV (November, 1946), 189.

New Yorker, XXII (August 24, 1946), 70.

Time, XLVIII (August 26, 1946), 98.

United States Quarterly Book List, II (December, 1946), 283-284.

All the King's Men. Toronto: George J. McLeod, Ltd., 1946. (Reissue.)

All the King's Men. London: Eyre & Spottiswoode Ltd., 1948. (Reissue.)

All the King's Men. New York: Grosset & Dunlap, Inc., 1948. (Reissue.)

All the King's Men. London: Eyre & Spottiswoode Ltd., 1950. (Reissue.)

All the King's Men. With a new introduction by the author. New York: Modern Library, 1953.

All the King's Men. With a new introduction by the author. Toronto: Random House of Canada, Ltd., 1953. (Reissue.)

All the King's Men. New York: Bantam Books, 1959. (A Bantam classic.) (Reissue.)

All the King's Men. Second edition. London: Eyre & Spottiswoode Ltd., 1960.

Signed Reviews

Jacobson, Dan. *Spectator*, CCIV (January 15, 1960), 83.
Price, R. G. G. *Punch*, CCXXXVIII (January 20, 1960), 139.

Unsigned Review

[London] *Times Literary Supplement*, January 15, 1960, p. 29.

All the King's Men. London: Landsborough Publications, Ltd., 1960. (Reissue.)

All the King's Men. With a new introduction by the author. New York: Time, Inc., 1963. (Time reading program special edition.)

Blackberry Winter. (Story.) A story illustrated by Wightman Williams. Cummington, Mass.: The Cummington Press, 1946.

The Circus in the Attic, and Other Stories. (Short stories.) First edition. New York: Harcourt, Brace, 1947.

Contents

"The Circus in the Attic"
"Blackberry Winter"
"When the Light Gets Green"

"Christmas Gift"
"Goodwood Comes Back"
"The Patented Gate and the Mean Hamburger"
"A Christian Education"
"The Love of Elsie Barton: A Chronicle"
"Testament of Flood"
"The Confession of Brother Grimes"
"Her Own People"
"The Life and Work of Professor Roy Millen"
"The Unvexed Isles"
"Prime Leaf"

Signed Review

Dedmon, Emmett, *Chicago Sunday Sun and Times—Book Week,* January 25, 1948, p. 5x.

* Eckman, Frederick. *Cronos,* No. 4 (1948), 75.

Elledge, Scott. *Furioso,* III (Spring, 1948), 81-82.

Farrelly, John. *New Republic,* CXVIII (January 26, 1948), 32.

Fiedler, Leslie A. *Kenyon Review,* X (Summer, 1948), 520, 525.

Frank, Joseph. *Hudson Review,* I (Summer, 1948), 284, 286, 288.

Fremantle, Anne. *Commonweal,* XLVII (March 12, 1948), 547.

Hicks, Granville. *New York Times Book Review,* January 25, 1948, pp. 5, 28.

Jackson, Joseph Henry. *San Francisco Chronicle,* February 3, 1948, p. 14.

Marshall, Margaret. *Nation,* CLXVI (February 21, 1948), 216.

Match, Richard. *New York Herald Tribune Weekly Book Review,* XXIV (January 25, 1948), 4.

O'Connor, William Van. *Western Review,* XII (Summer, 1948), 251-253.

Prescott, Orville. *Yale Review,* XXXVII (Spring, 1948), 575-576.

R., W. K. *Christian Science Monitor,* January 30, 1948, p. [14].

Smith, Henry Nash. *Saturday Review of Literature*, XXXI (January 31, 1948), 14-15.

Unsigned Reviews

Booklist, XLIV (February 15, 1948), 217.
New Yorker, XXIII (January 24, 1948), 80, 82.
Time, LI (January 26, 1948), 101.
United States Quarterly Book List, IV (June, 1948), 140.
Virginia Quarterly Review, XXIV (Autumn, 1948), cxviii.

The Circus in the Attic, and Other Stories. New York: Harcourt, Brace & Company, Inc., 1948. (Reissue.)

The Circus in the Attic, and Other Stories. Toronto: George J. McLeod, Ltd., 1948. (Reissue.)

The Circus in the Attic, and Other Stories. London: Eyre & Spottiswoode Ltd., 1952. (Reissue.)

The Circus in the Attic, and Other Stories. Toronto: George J. McLeod, Ltd., 1952. (Reissue.)

The Circus in the Attic. London: Eyre & Spottiswoode Ltd., 1956. (Reissue.)

The Circus in the Attic, and Other Stories. New York: Dell Publishing Company, 1959. (A Dell book, No. F82.) (Reissue.)

Modern Rhetoric. With readings. By Cleanth Brooks and Robert Penn Warren. (Textbook.) New York: Harcourt, Brace, 1949.

Signed Reviews

Dykema, K. W. *College English*, XII (October, 1950), 55-56.
Samuels, Ernest. *College English*, XII (October, 1950), 54-55.

Modern Rhetoric. By Cleanth Brooks and Robert Penn Warren. Second edition. New York: Harcourt, Brace, 1958.

Modern Rhetoric. By Cleanth Brooks and Robert Penn Warren. Shorter edition. New York: Harcourt, Brace & World, 1961.

Fundamentals of Good Writing: A Handbook of Modern Rhetoric. By Cleanth Brooks and Robert Penn Warren. (Textbook.) First edition. New York: Harcourt, Brace, 1950. (Text edition published in 1949 under title *Modern Rhetoric*.)

Signed Reviews

Stauffer, Donald A. *New Republic*, CXXIII (July 10, 1950), 21.

Stegner, Wallace. *New York Times Book Review*, LV (July 16, 1950), 5, 20.

Fundamentals of Good Writing: A Handbook of Modern Rhetoric. By Cleanth Brooks and Robert Penn Warren. London: Dennis Dobson, Ltd., 1952. (Reissue.)

Unsigned Review

[London] *Times Literary Supplement*, September 26, 1952, p. 630.

Fundamentals of Good Writing: A Handbook of Modern Rhetoric. By Cleanth Brooks and Robert Penn Warren. Toronto: George J. McLeod, Ltd., 1952. (Reissue.)

Fundamentals of Good Writing: A Handbook of Modern Rhetoric. By Cleanth Brooks and Robert Penn Warren. London: Dobson, 1956. (Reissue.)

World Enough and Time, A Romantic Novel. (Novel.) New York: Random House, 1950.

Signed Reviews

Baker, Carlos. *Virginia Quarterly Review*, XXVI (Autumn, 1950), 603-605.

Cowley, Malcolm. *New York Herald Tribune Book Review*, XXVI (June 25, 1950), 1.

Dedmon, Emmett. *Chicago Sunday Sun-Times*, June 25, 1950, sec. 2, p. 5.

Engle, Paul. *Chicago Sunday Tribune Magazine of Books*, June 25, 1950, p. 3.

Fiedler, Leslie. *Partisan Review*, XVII (September-October, 1950), 739-743.

Fowke, Edith. *Canadian Forum*, XXX (December, 1950), 214-215.

Gill, Brendan. *New Yorker*, XXVI (June 24, 1950), 89-90.

Guthrie, A. B. *Saturday Review of Literature*, XXXIII (June 24, 1950), 11-12.

Hatch, Robert. *New Republic*, CXXIII (July 31, 1950), 18-19.

Jackson, Joseph Henry. *San Francisco Chronicle*, June 26, 1950, p. 18.

Janeway, Elizabeth. *New York Times Book Review*, LV (June 25, 1950), 1, 22.

Jones, Ernest. *Nation*, CLXXI (July 8, 1950), 42.

McDonald, G. D. *Library Journal*, LXXV (May 1, 1950), 775.

Mizener, Arthur. *Kenyon Review*, XII (Autumn, 1950), 697-701.

Pickrel, Paul. *Yale Review*, XXXIX (Summer, 1950), 765-766.

Ridgely, Joseph V. *Hopkins Review*, IV (Fall, 1950), 61-63.

Rolo, C. J. *Atlantic Monthly*, CLXXXVI (July, 1950), 86-87.

Sandrock, Mary. *Catholic World*, CLXXI (August, 1950), 394.

Schiller, Andrew. *Western Review*, XV (Spring, 1951), 234-237.

Stoer, M. W. *Christian Science Monitor* [Magazine Section], July 1, 1950, p. 6.

Trese, L. J. *Commonweal*, LII (July 21, 1950), 373.

Unsigned Reviews

Booklist, XLVI (July 1, 1950), 336.

Bookmark (New York State Library), IX (June, 1950), 213.

* *Cleveland Open Shelf*, August, 1950, p. 16.

Time, LV (June 26, 1950), 98.

World Enough and Time. Toronto: Random House of Canada, Ltd., 1950. (Reissue.)

World Enough and Time. London: Eyre & Spottiswoode Ltd., 1951. (Reissue.)

World Enough and Time. New York: Garden City Books, 1951. (Reissue.)

An Anthology of Stories from the Southern Review. Edited by Cleanth Brooks and Robert Penn Warren. (Short stories.) Baton Rouge: Louisiana State University Press, 1953.

Brother to Dragons, A Tale in Verse and Voices. (Poem.) New York: Random House, 1953.

Signed Reviews

Ames, Alfred C. *Chicago Sunday Tribune Magazine of Books,* August 23, 1953, p. 3.

Bogan, Louise. *New Yorker,* XXIX (October 24, 1953), 157-158.

Deutsch, Babette. *New York Herald Tribune Book Review,* XXX (August 23, 1953), 3.

_______. *Yale Review,* XLIII (Winter, 1954), 276-279.

Edwards, John. *This World,* in *San Francisco Chronicle,* September 6, 1953, p. 18.

Fiedler, Leslie. *Partisan Review,* XXI (March-April, 1954), 208-212.

Flint, F. Cudworth. *Virginia Quarterly Review,* XXX (Winter, 1954), 143-148.

* Honig, Edwin. *Voices,* No. 154 (May-August, 1954), 41-44.

Jarrell, Randall. *New York Times Book Review,* LVIII (August 23, 1953), 6.

Joost, Nicholas. *Commonweal,* LIX (December 4, 1953), 231-232.

Kenner, Hugh. *Hudson Review,* VI (Winter, 1954), 605-610.

Lowell, Robert. *Kenyon Review,* XV (Autumn, 1953), 619-625.

McCormick, John. *Western Review*, XVIII (Winter, 1954), 163-167.

McDonald, G. D. *Library Journal*, LXXVIII (December 15, 1953), 2221.

O'Connor, William Van. *Sewanee Review*, LXII (Winter, 1954), 143-150.

Prescott, Orville. *New York Times* [daily], August 21, 1953, p. 15.

Schwartz, Delmore. *New Republic*, CXXIX (September 14, 1953), 17-18.

Swallow, Alan. *Talisman*, No. 4 (Winter, 1953), 38-42.

Tyler, Parker. *Poetry*, LXXXIII (December, 1953), 167-171.

Webster, H. C. *Saturday Review*, XXXVI (August 22, 1953), 11-12.

Unsigned Reviews

Booklist, L (September 15, 1953), 31.

Bookmark (New York State Library), XIII (October, 1953), 9.

Nation, CLXXVII (November 7, 1953), 376.

Time, LXII (August 24, 1953), 82.

Brother to Dragons: A Tale in Verse and Voices. Toronto: Random House of Canada, Ltd., 1953. (Reissue.)

Brother to Dragons: A Tale in Verse and Voices. London: Eyre & Spottiswoode Ltd., 1954. (Reissue.)

Signed Review

Kristol, Irving. *Encounter*, III (July, 1954), 74.

Short Story Masterpieces. Edited by Robert Penn Warren and Albert Erskine. (Short stories.) New York: Dell Books, 1954. (A Dell first edition, No. F16.)

Band of Angels. (Novel.) New York: Random House, 1955.

Signed Reviews

* Adams, Phoebe. *Atlantic Monthly*, CXCVI (September, 1955), 84-85.

Baker, Carlos. *Saturday Review*, XXXVIII (August 20, 1955), 9-10.

Benet, James. *San Francisco Chronicle*, August 31, 1955, p. 17.

Bradshaw, L. M. *Library Journal*, LXXX (August, 1955), 1699.

Brown, Ashley. *Shenandoah*, VII (Autumn, 1955), 87-91.

Coxe, L. O. *Yale Review*, XLV (Autumn, 1955), 159-160.

Craib, Roderick. *New Leader*, XXXVIII (September 26, 1955), 24-25.

Engle, Paul. *Chicago Sunday Tribune Magazine of Books*, August 21, 1955, p. 1.

Fiedler, Leslie. *New Republic*, CXXXIII (September 26, 1955), 28-30.

Geismar, Maxwell. *Nation*, CLXXXI (October 1, 1955), 287.

Hughes, Riley. *Catholic World*, CLXXXII (November, 1955), 147.

Lombardo, Agostino. *Lo Spettatore Italiano*, VIII (Dicembre, 1955), 528-530. (In Italian.)

McDowell, Frederick P. W. *Western Review*, XX (Winter, 1956), 167-171.

Mizener, Arthur. *New York Times Book Review*, LX (August 21, 1955), 1, 18.

Paulding, Gouverneur. *Reporter*, XIII (September 22, 1955), 46.

Prescott, Orville. *New York Times* [daily], August 22, 1955, p. 19.

R., C. F. *Springfield* [Massachusetts] *Republican*, September 4, 1955, p. 7c.

Rosenberger, Coleman. *New York Herald Tribune Book Review*, XXXII (August 21, 1955), 1, 6.

Scott, Nathan A., Jr. *Christian Century*, LXXIII (February 29, 1956), 272-273.

Sullivan, J. F. *Commonweal*, LXIII (November 11, 1955), 147-148.

Unsigned Reviews

Booklist, LII (September 1, 1955), 15.

Bookmark (New York State Library), XV (November, 1955), 37.

Time, LXVI (August 22, 1955), 86.

Band of Angels. London: Eyre & Spottiswoode Ltd., 1956. (Reissue.)

Signed Reviews

Scott-James, Marie. [London] *Sunday Times*, June 3, 1956, p. 5.

* Wain, John. *Observer*, June 3, 1956, p. 11.

Unsigned Review

[London] *Times*, May 31, 1956, p. 13.

Band of Angels. New York: New American Library of World Literature, 1956. (Reissue.)

Six Centuries of Great Poetry. Edited by Robert Penn Warren and Albert Erskine. (Poems.) New York: Dell Publishing Company, 1955. (A Dell first edition, No. FE69.)

Segregation, the Inner Conflict in the South. (Non-fiction.) New York: Random House, 1956.

Signed Reviews

Adams, Phoebe. *Atlantic Monthly*, CXCVIII (September, 1956), 83-84.

Brunn, Robert R. *Christian Science Monitor*, August 30, 1956, p. 7.

Clarke, M. M. *Catholic World*, CLXXXIV (November, 1956), 154-155.

Ethridge, Mark, Jr. *Saturday Review*, XXXIX (September 1, 1956), 14.

Furnas, J. C. *New York Herald Tribune Book Review*, XXXIII (September 2, 1956), 1.

Heimanson, R. H. *Library Journal*, LXXXI (September 15, 1956), 1998.

Hogan, William. *San Francisco Chronicle,* August 31, 1956, p. 17.

McGill, Ralph. *New York Times Book Review,* LXI (September 2, 1956), 1, 13.

Ottley, Roi. *Chicago Sunday Tribune Magazine of Books,* September 9, 1956, p. 3.

Pfaff, William. *Commonweal,* LXV (December 7, 1956), 268-269.

Potter, D. M. *Yale Review,* XLVI (Winter, 1957), 265.

Unsigned Reviews

Booklist and Subscription Books Bulletin, LIII (October 1, 1956), 62.

Bookmark (New York State Library), XVI (October, 1956), 8.

New Yorker, XXXII (October 13, 1956), 200.

Wisconsin Library Bulletin, LII (September-October, 1956), 209.

Segregation: the Inner Conflict in the South. Toronto: Random House of Canada, Ltd., 1956. (Reissue.)

Segregation: the Inner Conflict in the South. London: Eyre & Spottiswoode Ltd., 1957. (Reissue.)

Signed Reviews

MacKenzie, Norman. *New Statesman,* LIV (August 3, 1957), 154.

Singer, Marie B. *Twentieth Century,* CLXI (April, 1957), 395-397.

Unsigned Review

[London] *Times Literary Supplement,* March 29, 1957, p. 195.

Segregation, the Inner Conflict in the South. New York: Random House, 1956. (A Modern Library paperback, No. P30.) (Reissue.)

Segregation: the Inner Conflict in the South. Toronto: Random House of Canada, Ltd., 1957. (Paperback.) (Reissue.)

Segregation: the Inner Conflict in the South. New York: Vintage Books, 1961. (A Vintage book, No. V-145.) (Reissue.)

A New Southern Harvest, an Anthology. Edited by Robert Penn Warren and Albert Erskine. (Short stories.) New York: Bantam Books, 1957. (A Bantam book, No. F1556.)

Promises: Poems 1954-1956. (Poems.) New York: Random House, 1957.[1]

Contents

"To a Little Girl, One Year Old, in a Ruined Fortress"
- I. "Sirocco"
- II. "Gull's Cry"
- III. "The Child Next Door"
- IV. "The Flower"
- V. "Colder Fire"

"Promises"
- I. "What Was the Promise That Smiled from the Maples at Evening?"
- II. "Court-martial"
- III. "Gold Glade"
- IV. "Dark Woods"
  - 1. "Tonight the Woods Are Darkened"
  - 2. "The Dogwood"
  - 3. "The Hazel Leaf"
- V. "Country Burying (1919)"
- VI. "School Lesson Based on Word of Tragic Death of Entire Gillum Family"
- VII. "Summer Storm (Circa 1916), and God's Grace"
- VIII. "Founding Fathers, Nineteenth-Century Style, Southeast U.S.A."
- IX. "Foreign Shore, Old Woman, Slaughter of Octopus"
- X. "Dark Night of"
- XI. "Infant Boy at Midcentury"
  - 1. "When the Century Dragged"

[1] The *Catalog of Copyright Entries* indicates that this book was ". . . prev. pub. abroad 1957 & reg." However, the editor was unable to verify this assertion.

2. "Modification of Landscape"
3. "Brightness of Distance"

XII. "Lullaby: Smile in Sleep"

XIII. "Man in Moonlight"

1. "Moonlight Observed from Ruined Fortress"
2. "Walk by Moonlight in Small Town"
3. "Lullaby: Moonlight Lingers"

XIV. "Mad Young Aristocrat on Beach"

XV. "Dragon Country: To Jacob Boehme"

XVI. "Ballad of a Sweet Dream of Peace"

1. "And Don't Forget Your Corset Cover, Either"
2. "Keepsakes"
3. "Go It, Granny—Go It, Hog!"
4. "Friends of the Family, or Bowling a Sticky Cricket"
5. "You Never Knew Her Either, Though You Thought You Did, Inside Out"
6. "I Guess You Ought To Know Who You Are"
7. "Rumor Unverified Stop Can You Confirm Stop"

XVII. "Boy's Will, Joyful Labor without Pay, and Harvest Home (1918)"

1. "Morning"
2. "Work"
3. "The Snake"
4. "Hands Are Paid"

XVIII. "Lullaby: A Motion like Sleep"

XIX. "The Necessity for Belief"

Signed Reviews

Blum, Morgan. *Kenyon Review*, XXI (Winter, 1959), 97-120.

Casper, Leonard. *Western Review*, XXII (Autumn, 1957), 69-71.

Deutsch, Babette. *New York Herald Tribune Book Review*, XXXIV (August 25, 1957), 4.

Dickey, James. *Sewanee Review,* LXVI (Spring, 1958), 307-309.

Engle, Paul. *Chicago Sunday Tribune Magazine of Books,* September 8, 1957, p. 2.

Fitts, Dudley. *New York Times Book Review,* LXII (August 18, 1957), 6, 20.

Fjelde, Rolf. *Poetry,* XCII (April, 1958), 49-52.

Flint, F. Cudworth. *Virginia Quarterly Review,* XXXIV (Winter, 1958), 118-119.

Garrett, George Palmer. *The Georgia Review,* XII (Spring, 1958), 106-108.

McDonald, G. D. *Library Journal,* LXXXII (October 1, 1957), 2460.

M., J. *Voices,* No. 166 (May-August, 1958), 48-51.

R., S. *Saturday Review,* XL (November 9, 1957), 15, 42.

Rosenthal, M. L. *Nation,* CLXXXVI (January 18, 1958), 56-57.

Smith, W. J. *New Republic,* CXXXVII (October 14, 1957), 18-19.

Wasserstrom, William. *Prairie Schooner,* XXXII (Spring, 1958), 67-69.

Whittemore, Reed. *Yale Review,* XLVII (Winter, 1958), 284-285.

Unsigned Review

Booklist and Subscription Books Bulletin, LIV (October 1, 1957), 71.

Promises: Poems 1954-1956. Toronto: Random House of Canada, Ltd., 1957. (Reissue.)

Promises: Poems, 1954-1956. London: Eyre & Spottiswoode Ltd., 1959. (Reissue.)

Signed Reviews

Fuller, Roy. *London Magazine,* VI (August, 1959), 71.

Skelton, Robin. *New Statesman,* LVII (May 23, 1959), 732.

Remember the Alamo! (Non-fiction.) Illustrated by William Moyers. New York: Random House, 1958. (A Landmark book, No. 79.)

Signed Reviews

B., M. W. *Horn Book Magazine*, XXXIV (October, 1958), 392.

Graff, H. F. *New York Times Book Review*, LXIII (November 2, 1958), Pt. II, p. 3.

Maxwell, Emily. *New Yorker*, XXXIV (November 22, 1958), 214.

Taylor, Millicent. *Christian Science Monitor*, November 26, 1958, p. 19.

Unsigned Review

Booklist and Subscription Books Bulletin, LV (January 1, 1959), 245.

Remember the Alamo! Illustrated by William Moyers. (Landmark books to schools and school libraries only.) Eau Claire, Wis.: E. M. Hale & Company, 1958. (Reissue.)

Remember the Alamo! Illustrated by William Moyers. (Landmark books.) Toronto: Random House of Canada, Ltd., 1958. (Reissue.)

Selected Essays. (Essays.) New York: Random House, 1958.

Contents

"Pure and Impure Poetry" (1942)[2]

" 'The Great Mirage': Conrad and *Nostromo*" (1951)

"William Faulkner" (1946-50)

"Ernest Hemingway" (1944-47)

"The Themes of Robert Frost" (1947)

"Irony with a Center: Katherine Anne Porter" (1941-52)

"Love and Separateness in Eudora Welty" (1944)

"A Note on the Hamlet of Thomas Wolfe" (1935)

"Melville the Poet" (1945)

"A Poem of Pure Imagination: An Experiment in Reading" (1945-46)

Signed Reviews

Anderson, Charles. *Modern Language Notes*, LXXVI (January, 1961), 73-75.

[2] Unless otherwise noted, dates in parentheses following the titles of essays indicate the dates of composition of respective essays.

Casper, Leonard. *Western Review*, XXIII (Spring, 1959), 286-287.

Engle, Paul. *Chicago Sunday Tribune Magazine of Books*, July 13, 1958, p. 6.

Hynes, Sam. *Commonweal*, LXIX (October 3, 1958), 27-29.

Kazin, Alfred. *Partisan Review*, XXVI (Spring, 1959), 312, 314-316.

Pulos, C. E. *Prairie Schooner*, XXXIII (Spring, 1959), 1-2.

Redman, B. R. *Saturday Review*, XLI (July 19, 1958), 28.

Wermuth, P. C. *Library Journal*, LXXXIII (September 1, 1958), 2318.

Unsigned Reviews

Booklist and Subscription Books Bulletin, LV (November 1, 1958), 121.

New York Herald Tribune Book Review, XXXV (August 31, 1958), 10.

Selected Essays. London: Eyre & Spottiswoode Ltd., 1964. (Reissue.)

Signed Reviews

Cohen, Peter. *The Listener*, LXXI (February 27, 1964), 364.

Davie, Donald. *New Statesman*, LXVII (March 13, 1964), 406.

Igoe, W. J. *The Tablet*, CCXVIII (June 13, 1964), 666.

Tanner, Tony. *Spectator*, April 10, 1964, p. 492.

Unsigned Review

[London] *Times Literary Supplement*, April 9, 1964, p. 292.

The Cave. (Novel.) New York: Random House, 1959.

Signed Reviews

Abel, Lionel. *Commentary*, XXVIII (December, 1959), 541-544.

Allen, Charles A. *Arizona Quarterly*, XVI (Summer, 1960), 182-184.

*Arimond, Carroll. *Extension*, LIV (January, 1960), 6.

DeMott, Benjamin. *Hudson Review*, XII (Winter, 1959-60), 621-623.

Dorn, Norman K. *San Francisco Chronicle*, August 24, 1959, p. 33.

Engle, Paul. *Chicago Sunday Tribune Magazine of Books*, August 23, 1959, p. 1.

Hatch, Robert. *Nation*, CLXXXIX (September 12, 1959), 138-139.

Hicks, Granville. *Saturday Review*, XLII (August 22, 1959), 13.

Holmes, T. *Carleton Miscellany*, IV (Winter, 1963), 124-128.

Hughes, Riley. *Catholic World*, CXC (November, 1959), 127.

Hynes, Sam. *Commonweal*, LXX (September 4, 1959), 476-477.

Kiley, Frederick S. *Clearing House*, XXXV (March, 1961), 444.

Maddocks, Melvin. *Christian Science Monitor*, September 24, 1959, p. 9.

Malcolm, Donald. *New Yorker*, XXXV (October 31, 1959), 186, 189-190.

Martin, Terence. *New Republic*, CXLI (September 7, 1959), 20-21.

Mizener, Arthur. *New York Times Book Review*, LXIV (August 23, 1959), 1.

Nemerov, Howard. *Partisan Review*, XXVII (Winter, 1960), 176, 178-180, 183-184.

Prescott, Orville. *New York Times* [daily], August 24, 1959, p. 19.

Price, Martin. *Yale Review*, XLIX (Autumn, 1959), 124-126.

Pugh, Griffith T. *English Journal*, XLIX (February, 1960), 140.

Rolo, Charles. *Atlantic Monthly*, CCIV (October, 1959), 115-116.

Rosenberger, Coleman. *New York Herald Tribune Book Review*, XXXVI (August 23, 1959), 1.

Sandeen, Ernest. *Critic*, XVIII (October-November, 1959), 13, 63.
Slatoff, Walter. *Epoch*, X (Fall, 1959), 62-63.
Thompson, Frank H., Jr. *Prairie Schooner*, XXXV (Summer, 1961), 173-175.
Tick, Stanley, *Meanjin Quarterly*, XX, No. 1 (1961), 113-114.
Wermuth, P. C. *Library Journal*, LXXXIV (September 1, 1959), 2523-2524.

Unsigned Reviews

Booklist and Subscription Books Bulletin, LVI (September 15, 1959), 52.
Christian Century, LXXVI (November 11, 1959), 1315.
Kenyon Review, XXII (Winter, 1960), 166-167.
Time, LXXIV (August 24, 1959), 78-79.

The Cave. London: Eyre & Spottiswoode Ltd., 1959. ("First English edition.")

Signed Reviews

Coleman, John. *Spectator*, December 4, 1959, p. 836.
Gransden, K. W. *Encounter*, XIV (May, 1960), 78.
Shrapnel, Norman. *The Guardian* [Manchester], December 4, 1959, p. 13.
Waterhouse, Keith. *New Statesman*, LVIII (December 5, 1959), 816.

Unsigned Review

[London] *Times Literary Supplement*, November 27, 1959, p. 692.

The Gods of Mount Olympus. (Non-fiction.) Illustrated by William Moyers. New York: Random House, 1959. (A Legacy book, No. Y-1.)

The Gods of Mount Olympus. Illustrated by William Moyers. (Legacy book.) Toronto: Random House of Canada, Ltd., 1959. (Reissue.)

The Gods of Mount Olympus. Illustrated by William Moyers, (Legacy book.) London: Frederick Muller, Ltd., 1962. (Reissue.)

How Texas Won Her Freedom: The Story of Sam Houston and the Battle of San Jacinto. (Non-fiction.) San Jacinto Monument, Texas: San Jacinto Museum of History, 1959.

All the King's Men, a Play. (Play.) New York: Random House, 1960.

Signed Reviews

Freedley, George. *Library Journal,* LXXXV (July, 1960), 2615.

*Lipsett, Richard. *The Theatre,* II (May, 1960), 46.

Unsigned Review

Booklist and Subscription Books Bulletin, LVI (June 1, 1960), 596-597.

All the King's Men, a Play. New York: Dramatists Play Service, 1960. (Reissue.)

All the King's Men, a Play. Toronto: Random House of Canada, Ltd., 1960. (Reissue.)

"All the King's Men [a play]," *Sewanee Review,* LXVIII (Spring, 1960), 177-239. (Complete text.)

The Scope of Fiction. By Cleanth Brooks and Robert Penn Warren. (Textbook.) New York: Appleton-Century-Crofts, 1960. ("A shorter version of *Understanding Fiction.*")

You, Emperors, and Others: Poems, 1957-1960 (Poems.) New York: Random House, 1960.

Contents

"Garland for You"

1. "Clearly about You"
2. "Lullaby: Exercise in Human Charity and Self-Knowledge"
3. "Man in the Street"

4. "Switzerland"
5. "A Real Question Calling for Solution"
6. "The Letter about Money, Love, or Other Comfort, if Any"
7. "Arrogant Law"
8. "The Self that Stares"

"Two Pieces after Suetonius"

1. "Apology for Domitian"
2. "Tiberius on Capri"

"Mortmain"

1. "After Night Flight Son Reaches Bedside of Already Unconscious Father, Whose Right Hand Lifts in a Spasmodic Gesture, as though Trying to Make Contact: 1955"
2. "A Dead Language: Circa 1885"
3. "Fox-Fire: 1956"
4. "In the Turpitude of Time: N.D."
5. "A Vision: Circa 1880"

"Fatal Interview: Penthesilea and Achilles"

"Some Quiet, Plain Poems"

1. "Ornithology in a World of Flux"
2. "Holly and Hickory"
3. "The Well House"
4. "In Moonlight, Somewhere, They Are Singing"
5. "In Italian They Call the Bird *Civetta*"
6. "Debate: Question, Quarry, Dream"

"Ballad: Between the Boxcars"

1. "I Can't Even Remember the Name"
2. "He Was Formidable"
3. "He Has Fled"

"Two Studies in Idealism: Short Survey of American, and Human, History"

1. "Bear Track Plantation: Shortly after Shiloh"
2. "Harvard '61: Battle Fatigue"

"Nocturne: Traveling Salesman in Hotel Bedroom"

"So You Agree with What I Say? Well, What Did I Say?"

"Prognosis: A Short Story, the End of Which You Will Know Soon Enough"

1. "And Oh—"
2. "What the Sand Said"
3. "What the Joree Said, the Joree Being Only a Bird"

"Autumnal Equinox on Mediterranean Beach"

"Nursery Rhymes"

1. "Knockety-Knockety-Knock"
2. "News of Unexpected Demise of Little Boy Blue"
3. "Mother Makes the Biscuits"
4. "The Bramble Bush"

"Short Thoughts for Long Nights"

1. "Nightmare of Mouse"
2. "Nightmare of Man"
3. "Colloquy with Cockroach"
4. "Little Boy on Voyage"
5. "Obsession"
6. "Joy"
7. "Cricket, on Kitchen Floor, Enters History"
8. "Little Boy and General Principle"
9. "Grasshopper Tries to Break Solipsism"

Signed Reviews

Engle, Paul. *Chicago Sunday Tribune Magazine of Books*, September 4, 1960, p. 7.

Fitts, Dudley. *New York Times Book Review*, LXV (October 23, 1960), 32.

Hardy, John E. *Poetry*, XCIX (October, 1961), 58-62.

Hartman, Geoffrey H. *Kenyon Review*, XXIII (Spring, 1961), 356-357.

*Hazo, S. *Poetry Dial*, I. No. 2 (Spring, 1961), 45-46.

Holmes, John. *New York Herald Tribune Book Review*, XXXVII (October 16, 1960), 12.

Martz, Louis L. *Yale Review*, L (Spring, 1961), 445-446.

Morse, Samuel F. *Virginia Quarterly Review*, XXXVII (Spring, 1961), 295-296.

Robie, Burton A. *Library Journal*, LXXXV (October 15, 1960), 3664.

Thompson, John. *Hudson Review*, XIII (Winter, 1960-61), 619-620.

Zinnes, Harriet. *Prairie Schooner*, XXXVI (Spring, 1962), 85-87.

Unsigned Review

Booklist and Subscription Books Bulletin, LVII (September 1, 1960), 17.

Conversations on the Craft of Poetry. By Cleanth Brooks and Robert Penn Warren, with Robert Frost and others. (Textbook.) New York: Holt, Rinehart and Winston, 1961. ("A transcript of the tape recording made to accompany *Understanding Poetry*, Third edition.")

The Legacy of the Civil War: Meditations on the Centennial. (Non-fiction.) New York: Random House, 1961.

Signed Reviews

Brunn, Robert R. *Christian Science Monitor*, May 1, 1961, p. [13].

Donald, David. *New York Times Book Review*, LXVI (May 14, 1961), Pt. I, p. 3.

Harwell, Richard. *Chicago Sunday Tribune Magazine of Books*, April 23, 1961, p. 6.

Heaps, Willard A. *Library Journal*, LXXXVI (May 15, 1961), 1884-1885.

Hogan, William. *San Francisco Chronicle*, April 14, 1961, p. 31.

Jones, Peter d'A. *New Republic*, CXLIV (May 15, 1961), 16-17.

Kazin, Alfred. *Reporter*, XXIV (June 8, 1961), 40, 42-44. Reprinted in *Contemporaries*. By Alfred Kazin. Boston: Little, Brown and Company, 1962, pp. 178-183.

McNaspy, C. J. *America*, CV (April 15, 1961), 155-156.

Poore, Charles. *New York Times* [daily], April 27, 1961, p. 19.

Rubin, Louis D., Jr. *Sewanee Review*, LXIX (Summer, 1961), 500-506. [Response to Kazin's review in *Reporter*.]

Tobin, Richard L. *Saturday Review*, XLIV (July 8, 1961), 23.

Weaver, Richard M. *National Review*, X (June 17, 1961), 389-390.

Wight, Willard E. *Civil War History*, VIII (September, 1962), 337.

Unsigned Reviews

Booklist and Subscription Books Bulletin, LVII (May 15, 1961), 567.

New Yorker, XXXVII (April 29, 1961), 150.

Tennessee Historical Quarterly, XX (September, 1961), 285-286.

The Legacy of the Civil War: Meditations on the Centennial. Toronto: Random House of Canada, Ltd., 1961. (Reissue.)

The Legacy of the Civil War: Meditations on the Centennial. New York: Vintage Books Inc., 1964. (Paperback.) (Reissue.)

Signed Review

Burger, N. K. *New York Times Book Review*, LXX (January 31, 1965), 43.

Wilderness: A Tale of the Civil War. (Novel.) New York: Random House, 1961.

Signed Reviews

Adams, Phoebe. *Atlantic Monthly*, CCVIII (December, 1961), 126.

Bowen, Robert O. *National Review*, XI (December 2, 1961), 383.

Butcher, Fanny. *Chicago Sunday Tribune Magazine of Books*, November 19, 1961, pp. 1-2.

Gardiner, Harold C. *America*, CVI (November 11, 1961), 206.

Gerard, David. *Civil War Times*, III (February, 1962), 20.

Hartt, J. N. *Yale Review*, LI (Winter, 1962), 304.

Hertz, Robert N. *New Republic*, CXLV (December 18, 1961), 23.

Hicks, Granville. *Saturday Review*, XLIV (November 18, 1961), 19.

Hyman, Stanley E. *New Leader,* XLIV (November 13, 1961), 24-25.

Hynes, Samuel. *New York Times Book Review,* LXVI (November 19, 1961), 58.

Jackson, Katherine G. *Harper's,* CCXXIV (January, 1962), 96.

Kleine, Don W. *Epoch,* XI (Winter, 1962), 263-268.

Lacy, Bernard. *Christian Century,* LXXVIII (December 20, 1961), 1531.

McMichael, George. *This World,* in *San Francisco Sunday Chronicle,* January 7, 1962, pp. 17-18.

Magmer, James. *Catholic World,* CXCIV (January, 1962), 244-245.

*Moore, L. H. *Critique: Studies in Modern Fiction,* VIII (Winter, 1965-1966), 75.

Nyren, Dorothy. *Library Journal,* LXXXVI (December 15, 1961), 4309.

Prescott, Orville. *New York Times* [daily], November 15, 1961, p. 41.

Pugh, Griffith T. *English Jounral,* LI (May, 1962), 374.

Rosenberger, Coleman. *New York Herald Tribune (Christmas) Books,* XXXVIII (December 3, 1961), 4.

Sale, Roger. *Hudson Review,* XV (Spring, 1962), 134-135.

Wilson, James R. *Books Abroad,* XXXVI (Winter, 1962), 81-82.

Unsigned Reviews

Booklist and Subscription Books Bulletin, LVIII (December 1, 1961), 226-227.

Bookmark (New York State Library), XXI (May, 1962), 224.

Newsweek, LVIII (November 20, 1961), 109.

Time, LXXVIII (November 17, 1961), 93.

Virginia Quarterly Review, XXXVIII (Winter, 1962), viii.

Wilderness: A Tale of the Civil War. London: Eyre & Spottiswoode Ltd., 1962. (Reissue.)

Signed Reviews

Adams, Jennifer. *Time & Tide*, XLIII (May 31, 1962), 32.
Bellasis, M. *The Tablet*, CCXVI (August 18, 1962), 768.
Daniel, John. *Spectator*, June 22, 1962, p. 834.
Price, R. G. G. *Punch*, CCXLII (June 20, 1962), 954.
Richardson, Maurice. *New Statesman*, LXIII (June 1, 1962), 804.
Shrapnel, Norman. *The Guardian* [Manchester], June 1, 1962, p. 7.

Unsigned Reviews

[London] *Times Literary Supplement*, June 1, 1962, p. 385.
The Times Weekly Review, June 7, 1962, p. 10.

Wilderness: A Tale of the Civil War. New York: New American Library of World Literature, 1962. (A Signet book, No. P2231.) (Reissue.)

Flood, a Romance of Our Time. (Novel.) New York: Random House, 1964.

Signed Reviews

Baker, Carlos. *Book Week* [The Sunday *Herald Tribune*], I (April 26, 1964), 6, 10.
Barrett, William. *Atlantic Monthly*, CCXIII (June, 1964), 134.
Crews, F. C. *New York Times Book Review*, April 26, 1964, p. 6.
Davenport, Guy. *National Review*, XVI (July 14, 1964), 609-610.
DeMott, Benjamin. *Reporter*, XXXI (July 2, 1964), 34, 36-37.
Dolbier, Maurice. *New York Herald Tribune* [daily], April 24, 1964, p. 23.
Fadiman, Clifton. *Book-of-the-Month Club News*, May, 1964, pp. 12-13.
Gaines, E. J. *Library Journal*, LXXXIX (May 15, 1964), 2117.
Gardiner, Helen C. *America*, CX (June 13, 1964), 826.

Hardy, John Edward. *Virginia Quarterly Review*, XL (Summer, 1964), 485-489.
Hicks, Granville. *Saturday Review*, XLVII (April 25, 1964), 29-30.
Longley, John L., Jr. *Southern Review*, n. s. I (Autumn, 1965), 974-980.
Mizener, Arthur. *Sewanee Review*, LXXII (Autumn, 1964), 690-698.
*Oppenheim, Jane. *Best Sellers*, XXIV (June 1, 1964), 104.
Poore, Charles. *New York Times* [daily], April 23, 1964, p. 37.
Stewart, J. L. *Yale Review*, LIV (Winter, 1965), 252-258.
Sullivan, Richard. *Books Today—Chicago Sunday Tribune*, May 3, 1964, pp. 6-7.
Wain, John. *New Republic*, CL (May 16, 1964), 23-25.
West, Anthony. *New Yorker*, XL (September 12, 1964), 204-205.

Unsigned Reviews

Newsweek, LXIII (May 4, 1964), 93.
Time, LXXXIII (April 24, 1964), 106.

Flood. London: William Collins Sons & Co., Ltd., 1964. (Reissue.)

Signed Reviews

Hugh-Jones, Stephen. *New Statesman*, LXVIII (October 30, 1964), 666.
Richler, Mordecai. *Spectator*, October 30, 1964, p. 581.

Unsigned Review

[London] *Times Literary Supplement*, November 5, 1964, p. 993.

Flood: A Romance of Our Time. New York: William Collins Sons & Co., Ltd., 1964. (Reissue.)

Who Speaks for the Negro? (Non-fiction.) New York: Random House, 1965.

Signed Reviews

Cheney, Brainard. *Sewanee Review*, LXXIV (Spring, 1966), 545-550.

Dolbier, Maurice. *New York Herald Tribune*, May 28, 1965, p. 19.
Epstein, Joseph. *Commentary*, XL (October, 1965), 101-105.
Footlick, Jerrold K. *National Observer*, July 19, 1965, p. 19.
F[uller], H[oyt] W. *Negro Digest*, XV (December, 1965), 93.
Gallagher, J. J. *America*, CXIII (July 10, 1965), 60, 62.
Galphin, Bruce. *Saturday Review*, XLVIII (June 5, 1965), 22.
Gaston, Paul M. *Virginia Quarterly Review*, XLI (Autumn, 1965), 618.
Handlin, Oscar. *New York Times Book Review*, July 4, 1965, p. 3.
Haselden, Kyle. *Christian Century*, LXXXII (October 6, 1965), 1235-1236.
Hays, F. *Carleton Miscellany*, VI (Fall, 1965), 69-72.
Kaledin, Arthur. *Commonweal*, LXXXIII (December 24, 1965), 377-379.
Karpatkin, Marvin M. *Nation*, CCII (January 31, 1966), 134-136.
M[addocks], M[elvin]. *Christian Science Monitor*, July 1, 1965, p. [9].
Meier, August. *Dissent*, XII (Autumn, 1965), 509-511.
Murray, A. *New Leader*, XLVIII (June 21, 1965), 25-27.
Poore, Charles. *New York Times* [daily], CXIV (June 1, 1965), 37.
———. *New York Times* [daily], CXIV (June 8, 1965), 39.
Rabinowitz, V. *Science and Society*, XXIX (Fall, 1965), 458-459.
Raines, C. A. *Library Journal*, XC (September 1, 1965), 3469-3470.
Tolson, M. B. *Book Week* [The Sunday *Herald Tribune*], II (May 30, 1965), 5.
Weeks, Edward. *Atlantic Monthly*, CCXVI (July, 1965), 137.

Woodward, C. Vann. *New Republic*, CLII (May 22, 1965), 21-23.

Unsigned Reviews

Booklist and Subscription Books Bulletin, LXI (July 15, 1965), 1044.

Choice: Books for College Libraries, II (October, 1965), 538.

Library Journal, XC (September 15, 1965), 3819.

New Yorker, XLI (June 19, 1965), 126-127.

Newsweek, LXV (June 7, 1965), 84-86.

Who Speaks for the Negro? New York: Vintage Books, 1966. (Paperback.) (Reissue.)

Unsigned Reviews

Publishers' Weekly, CLXXXIX (January 10, 1966), 90.

Saturday Review, XLIX (April 23, 1966), 51.

Who Speaks for the Negro? Toronto: Random House of Canada, Ltd., 1966. (Paperback.) (Reissue.)

Faulkner: A Collection of Critical Essays. Edited by Robert Penn Warren. (Essays.) Englewood Cliffs, N. J.: Prentice-Hall, 1966. (A Spectrum book: Twentieth Century Views.) (Paperback and hardback.)

Signed Reviews

Hicks, Granville. *Saturday Review*, L (May 6, 1967), 27-28.

Merton, Thomas. *Critic*, XXV (April-May, 1967), 76-80.

Raines, C. A. *Library Journal*, XCII (January 15, 1967), 243.

Unsigned Review

Booklist and Subscription Books Bulletin, LXIII (April 1, 1967), 831.

A Plea in Mitigation: Modern Poetry and the End of an Era. (Essay.) Macon, Ga.: Wesleyan College, 1966. (Eugenia Dorothy Blount Lamar lecture, 1966.)

Selected Poems, New and Old, 1923-1966. (Poems.) New York: Random House, 1966.

Contents

TALE OF TIME
New Poems 1960-1966

(2. "The Bear and the Last Person to Remember")
(3. "The Human Fabric")
(4. "Afterwards")

"The Day Dr. Knox Did It"
I. "Place and Time"
II. "The Event"
III. "A Confederate Veteran Tries to Explain the Event"
IV. "The Place Where the Boy Pointed"
V. "And All That Came Thereafter"

"Holy Writ"
I. "Elijah on Mount Carmel"
II. "Saul at Gilboa"

"Delight"
I. "Into Broad Daylight"
II. "Love: Two Vignettes"
1. "Mediterranean Beach, Day after Storm"
2. "Deciduous Spring"
III. "Something Is Going to Happen"
IV. "Dream of a Dream the Small Boy Had"
V. "Two Poems About Suddenly and a Rose"
1. "Dawn"
2. "Intuition"
VI. "Not to Be Trusted"
VII. "Finisterre"

From YOU, EMPERORS, AND OTHERS
Poems 1957-1960

"Garland for You"
I. "Clearly About You"
II. "The Letter About Money, Love, or Other Comfort, if Any"
III. "Man in the Street"
IV. "Switzerland"
V. "A Real Question Calling for Solution"
VI. "Arrogant Law"

"Two Pieces after Suetonius"

I. "Apology for Domitian"

II. "Tiberius on Capri"

"Mortmain"

I. "After Night Flight Son Reaches Bedside of Already Unconscious Father, Whose Right Hand Lifts in a Spasmodic Gesture, as Though Trying to Make Contact: 1955"

II. "A Dead Language: Circa 1885"

III. "Fox Fire: 1956"

IV. "In the Turpitude of Time: N.D."

V. "A Vision: Circa 1880"

"Some Quiet, Plain Poems"

I. "Ornithology in a World of Flux"

II. "Holly and Hickory"

III. "The Well House"

IV. "In Moonlight, Somewhere, They Are Singing"

V. "In Italian They Call the Bird *Civetta*"

VI. "Debate: Question, Quarry, Dream"

"Ballad: Between the Boxcars (1923)"

I. "I Can't Even Remember the Name"

II. "He Was Formidable"

"Two Studies in Idealism: Short Survey of American, and Human, History"

I. "Bear Track Plantation: Shortly After Shiloh"

II. "Harvard '61: Battle Fatigue"

"Autumnal Equinox on Mediterranean Beach"

"Nursery Rhymes"

I. "Knockety-Knockety-Knock"

II. "News of Unexpected Demise of Little Boy Blue"

III. "Mother Makes the Biscuits"

"Short Thoughts for Long Nights"

I. "Nightmare of Mouse"

II. "Colloquy with Cockroach"

III. "Cricket, on Kitchen Floor, Enters History"

IV. "Grasshopper Tries to Break Solipsism"

From PROMISES
Poems 1954-1956

"To a Little Girl, One Year Old, in a Ruined Fortress"
- I. "Sirocco"
- II. "Gull's Cry"
- III. "The Child Next Door"
- IV. "The Flower'
- V. "Colder Fire"

"Promises"
- I. "What Was the Promise That Smiled from the Maples at Evening?"
- II. "Court-Martial"
- III. "Gold Glade"
- IV. "Dark Woods"
  1. "Tonight the Woods Are Darkened"
  2. "The Dogwood"
  3. "The Hazel Leaf"
- V. "Country Burying (1919)"
- VI. "School Lesson Based on Word of Tragic Death of Entire Gillum Family"
- VII. "Summer Storm (Circa 1916), and God's Grace"
- VIII. "Founding Fathers, Nineteenth-Century Style, Southeast U.S.A."
- IX. "Foreign Shore, Old Woman, Slaughter of Octopus"
- X. "Dark Night of the Soul"
- XI. "Infant Boy at Midcentury"
  1. "When the Century Dragged"
  2. "Modification of Landscape"
  3. "Brightness of Distance"
- XII. "Lullaby: Smile in Sleep"
- XIII. "Man in Moonlight"
  1. "Moonlight Observed from Ruined Fortress"
  2. "Walk by Moonlight in Small Town"
  3. "Lullaby: Moonlight Lingers"
- XIV. "Mad Young Aristocrat on Beach"

XV. "Dragon Country: To Jacob Boehme"
XVI. "Ballad of a Sweet Dream of Peace"
1. "And Don't Forget Your Corset Cover, Either"
2. "Keepsakes"
3. "Go It, Granny—Go It, Hog!"
4. "Friends of the Family, or Bowling a Sticky Cricket"
5. "You Never Knew Her Either, Though You Thought You Did"
6. "I Guess You Ought to Know Who You Are"
7. "Rumor Unverified Stop Can You Confirm Stop"
XVII. "Boy's Will, Joyful Labor Without Pay, and Harvest Home (1918)"
1. "Morning"
2. "Work"
3. "The Snake"
4. "Hands Are Paid"
XVIII. "Lullaby: A Motion Like Sleep"

From SELECTED POEMS
1923-1943

"The Ballad of Billie Potts"
"Terror"
"Pursuit"
"Original Sin: A Short Story"
"Crime"
"Letter from a Coward to a Hero"
"History"
"End of Season"
"Ransom"
"To a Friend Parting"
"Eidolon"
"Revelation"
"Mexico Is a Foreign Country: Four Studies in Naturalism"

I. "Butterflies over the Map"
II. "The World Comes Galloping: A True Story"
III. "Small Soldiers with Drum in Large Landscape"
IV. "The Mango on the Mango Tree"
"Monologue at Midnight"
"Bearded Oaks"
"Picnic Remembered"
"Love's Parable"
"Late Subterfuge"
"Man Coming of Age"
"The Garden"
"The Return: An Elegy"
"Kentucky Mountain Farm"
I. "Rebuke of the Rocks"
II. "At the Hour of the Breaking of the Rocks"
III. "History Among the Rocks"
IV. "The Return"
"Pondy Woods"
"Letter of a Mother"
"To a Face in a Crowd"

Signed Reviews

Burke, H. C. *Library Journal*, XCI (September 1, 1966), 3962.

Carruth, H. *Hudson Review*, XIX (Winter, 1966-67), 693-694.

Davison, Peter. *Atlantic Monthly*, CCXVIII (November, 1966), 163.

Garrigue, Jean. *New Leader*, L (March 27, 1967), 25.

Gelpi, Albert J. *Christian Science Monitor*, January 19, 1967, p. 11.

Gold, Arthur R. *Book Week* [Sunday *World Journal Tribune*], October 23, 1966, p. 15.

Kennedy, William. *National Observer*, February 6, 1967, p. 31.

Martz, L. L. *Yale Review*, LVI (Winter, 1967), 275-279.

Rubin, Louis D., Jr., *New York Times Book Review*, October 9, 1966, p. 4.

Slater, Joseph. *Saturday Review*, XLIX (December 31, 1966), 24-25.

Spector, R. D. *Saturday Review*, L (February 11, 1967), 39.

Stafford, William. *Books Today* [*Chicago Sunday Tribune*], October 9, 1966, p. 10.

Wain, John. *New Republic*, CLV (November 26, 1966), 16-18.

Unsigned Reviews

Booklist and Subscription Books Bulletin, LXIII (December 1, 1966), 401.

Choice, III (January, 1967), 1018.

Virginia Quarterly Review, XLIII (Winter, 1967), xvii.

Randall Jarrell, 1914-1965. Edited by Robert Lowell, Peter Taylor, and Robert Penn Warren. (Non-fiction.) New York: Farrar, Straus & Giroux, 1967.

II. Translations of Warren's Books

All the King's Men

Alla Kungens Män. Översättning av Nils Holmberg. Stockholm: Bonnier, 1947.

Alle Kongens Maend. Annobeth Kruuse. København: Grafisk Forlag, 1948.

Alle Kongens Menn. Fredrik Wulfsberg. Oslo: Gyldendahl, 1948.

Des Königs Tross. Ilse Krämer. Zürich: Büchergilde Gutenberg, 1949.

Tutti Gli Uomini Del Re. Luigi Berti. Milano: Bompiani, 1949.

Decepción [novela]. Buenos Aires: Ediciones Antonio Zamora, [1950]. (Versión castellana de Juan Rodríguez Chicano).

Les Fous Du Roi. Pierre Singer. Paris: Delamain et Boutelleau, 1950.

Les Fous Du Roi. Pierre Singer. Paris: Le Club Français du Livre, 1951.

Der Gouverneur. Ilse Krämer. Hamburg: Krüger, 1951.

Zij Gaven Hem Macht. J. G. Elburg & M. Mok. Amsterdam: De Bezige Bij, 1951.

Kol Anshey Ha-Melekh. A. Ben-Dan. Tel-Aviv: Idit, 1954.

Der Gouverneur. Ilse Krämer. München: Goldmann, 1956.

İktîdar Hirsi. Nermin Türkmen. İstanbul: Türkiye Yayinevi, 1958.

Gubernator. Przełozył Bronisław Zieliński. Warszawa: Państwowy Instytut Wydawniczy, 1960.

Svi Kraljevi Ljudi. Preveo Stjepan Krešić. Zagreb: Naprijed, 1960.

Gubernator. Bronisław Zieliński. Wwa: Państw. Instytut Wydawn. (Wyd. 2), 1962.

Gubernator (T. 1-2). Bronisław Zieliński. Wwa: Państw. Instytut Wydawn. (Wyd. 3), 1964. 2v.

All the King's Men, a Play

Blut auf dem Mond: ein Schauspiel in 3 Akten von Robert Penn Warren, in der Bühnenbearbeitung von Erwin Piscator. Deutsche Fassung von Erwin Piscator und Hellmut Schlien. Emsdetten (Westf.) Lechte, 1957.

At Heaven's Gate

Alle Porte Del Cielo. L. Panella Coggi. Milano: Baldini e Castoldi, 1948.

Aux Portes Du Ciel. Jean-Gérard Chauffeteau. Paris: Delamain et Boutelleau, 1952.

Band of Angels

Slavin Van De Vrijheid. C. J. Kelk. Amsterdam: Elsevier, 1956.

Slavin Van De Vrijheid. Cornelis Jan Kelk. Brussel: Elsevier, 1956.

Amantha. Helmut Degner. Gütersloh: Bertelsmann, 1957.

La Banda Degli Angeli. Bruno Oddera. Milano: Bompiani, 1957.

Coro De Ángeles. J. M. Alinari. Bs. As.: Kraft, 1957.

L'Esclave Libre. J.-G. Chauffeteau & Gilbert Vivier. Paris: Stock, 1957.

L'Esclave Libre. Jean-Gérard Chauffeteau & Gilbert Vivier. Paris: Club des éditeurs, 1957.

Om Jeg Blot Kunne Blive Fri. Karina Windfeld-Hansen. København: Grafisk Forlag, 1957.

Tenshi No Mure. (Gendai Amerika Bungaku Zenshû, 10). Yoshihiro Nabeshima; Ryo Namikawa. Tokyo: Arechi Shuppansha, 1957.

Četa Andjela. Boris Gerechtshammer. Rijeka: Otokar Keršovani, 1958.

Amantha. Helmut Degner. Güterloh: Bertelsmann Lesering, 1959.

Havurat Maleakhim. Moshe Ben-Refael. Tel-Aviv: Idit, 1959.

Havurat Mal'akim. M. Ben Rafael. Tel-Aviv: Iddit, 1964.

The Cave

La Caverna. Elsa Pelitti. Milano: Bompiani, 1960.

Le Caverne. Connie Fennell. Paris: Stock, 1960.

Die Höhle von Johntown: Roman. Helmut Degner. Gütersloh, Ger.: S. Mohn, 1961.

La Caverna. Versión castellana de Josefina Martinez Alinari. Buenos Aires: Guillermo Kraft, 1962.

Pećina. Omer Lakomica. Rijeka: Otokar Keršovani, 1963.

The Circus in the Attic

Il Circo in Soffitta. Bruno Oddera. Milano: Bompiani, 1959.

Shûkyô Kyôiku, etc. Tamotsu Hashiguchi. Tokyo: Nan'un-dô, 1960.

The Legacy of the Civil War

L'Héritage De La Guerre Civile. Pierre Singer. Paris: Stock, 1962.

Night Rider

Hovslag I Natten. Karina Windfeld-Hansen. København: Grafisk Forlag, 1949.

Le Cavalier de la Nuit, Roman. Traduit de l'américain par Michel

Mohrt. Avant-propos à l'édition française par l'auteur. Paris: Librairie Stock, 1951.

Il Cavaliere Della Notte. Maria Stella Ferrari. Milano: Bompiani, 1954.

O Cavaleiro Da Noite. João B. Viegas. Lisboa: Cor, 1959.

El Caballero De La Noche. E. Piñas. Barcelona: Plaza & Janés, 1960.

El Caballero De La Noche. E. Piñas. Barcelona: Plaza & Janés, 1963.

Remember the Alamo!

Slaget om Fort Alamo. Margareta Schlyter-Stiernstedt. Sthlm: B. Wahlström, 1965.

Segregation

Ségrégation. (Essai sur le problème noir en Amérique.) Jean-Luc Salvador. Paris: Stock, 1957.

Selected Essays

Ausgewählte Essays. Hans Hennecke & Hans Walz. Gütersloh: S. Mohn, 1961.

Short Story Masterpieces

Hyeondae Yeongmi Danpyeonseon. Byeong-taeg Yang & Ga-hyeong Lee. Seoul: Euryumunhwasa, 1961.

Wilderness

La Grande Forêt. Jean-G. Chauffeteau & Gilbert Vivier. Paris: Stock, 1962.

Puszcza. Opowieść z czasów wojny domowej. Bronisław Zieliński. Wwa: Państw. Instytut Wydawn., 1964.

World Enough and Time

Nog Av Tid Och Rum. (En Romantisk Berättelse.) Nils Holmberg. Stockholm: Albert Bonniers förlag, 1951.

Det Store Bedrag. Erling Sundve. Oslo: Gyldendal, 1952.

La Vida Esdifícil [*una Novela Romántica.* Santiago de Chile]: Zig-zag, [1952]. (Traductora: Lilian Lorca.)

Nel Vortice Del Tempo. Glauco Cambon. Milano-Verona: Mondadori, 1954.

Le Grand Souffle. J.-G. Chauffeteau & Gilbert Vivier. Paris: Delamain et Boutelleau, 1955.

Het Verleden Laat Niet Los. Jean H. P. Jacobs. Antw.: P. Vinck, 1957.

Intikam Hirsi. Sevinç Değer. İstanbul: Türkiye Yayinevi, 1958.

III. Short Stories

*Black Is Not the Color of My True Love's Hair," *Esquire*, September, 1959, p. 112. [An excerpt from *The Cave.*]

"Blackberry Winter," *Blackberry Winter*. A story illustrated by Wightman Williams. [Cummington, Mass.]: The Cummington Press, 1946, pp. 7-49;
The Circus in the Attic, and Other Stories, pp. 63-87.

"Cass Mastern's Wedding Ring," *Partisan Review*, XI (Fall, 1944), 375-407. [An excerpt from chapter four of *All the King's Men.*]

"A Christian Education," *Mademoiselle*, XX (January, 1945), 96-97, 155-157;
The Circus in the Attic, and Other Stories, pp. 134-142.

"Christmas Gift," *Virginia Quarterly Review*, XIII (Winter, 1937), 73-85;

The Circus in the Attic, and Other Stories, pp. 96-107.

*The Circus in the Attic," *Cosmopolitan*, CXXIII September, 1947), 67-70, 73-74, 76, 78, 80, 83-84, 86, 88;
The Circus in the Attic, and Other Stories, pp. 3-62.

*"The Confession of Brother Grimes," *Cronos*, I (Fall, 1947), 29-30;
The Circus in the Attic, and Other Stories, pp. 170-174.

"The Destiny of Hamish Bond," *Sewanee Review*, LXIII (Summer, 1955), 349-381. [Excerpt from *Band of Angels.*]

"The Fiddlersburg Preacher," *Esquire*, LX (July, 1963), 55-56.

[Excerpt from the first draft of *Flood, a Romance of Our Time.*]

"Goodwood Comes Back," *Southern Review,* VI (Winter, 1941), 526-536;
The Circus in the Attic, and Other Stories, pp. 108-119.

"Have You Seen Sukie?" *Virginia Quarterly Review,* XXXIX (Autumn, 1963), 574-586.

"Her Own People," *Virginia Quarterly Review,* XI (April, 1935), 289-304;
The Circus in the Attic, and Other Stories, pp. 175-189.

"How Willie Proudfit Came Home," *Southern Review,* IV (1938-39), 299-321.

"It's a Long Way from Central Park to Fiddlersburg," *Kenyon Review,* XXVI (Winter, 1964), 129-143.

"The Life and Work of Professor Roy Millen," *Mademoiselle,* XVI (February, 1943), 88, 145-149;
The Circus in the Attic, and Other Stories, pp. 190-198.

"Love and Death in Johntown, Tenn.," *Partisan Review,* XXVI (Summer, 1959), 392-419. [Excerpt from *The Cave.*]

"The Love of Elsie Barton: A Chronicle," *Mademoiselle,* XXII (February, 1946), 161, 282-290;
The Circus in the Attic, and Other Stories, pp. 143-162.

"Moths Against the Screen," *Saturday Evening Post,* CCXXXVII (April 4, 1964), 42-43, 46-50, 52-55. [Excerpt from *Flood, a Romance of Our Time.*]

"The Natural History of Ikey Sumpter, Formerly of Johntown, Tenn.," *Sewanee Review,* LXVII (Summer, 1959), 347-400. [Excerpt from *The Cave.*]

"The Patented Gate and the Mean Hamburger," *Mademoiselle,* XXIV (January, 1947), 188-189, 242-243, 245-246;
The Circus in the Attic, and Other Stories, pp. 120-133.

"Portrait of La Grand' Bosse," *Kenyon Review*, XII (Winter, 1950), 41-50. [Excerpt from *World Enough and Time.*]

"Prime Leaf," *American Caravan* IV. Edited by Alfred Kreymborg, Lewis Mumford, and Paul Rosenfeld. New York: Macaulay Company, 1931, pp. 3-61;
The Circus in the Attic, and Other Stories, pp. 211-276.

"Statement of Ashby Wyndham," *Sewanee Review*, LI (Spring, 1943), 183-236. [Excerpt from *At Heaven's Gate.*]

"Testament of Flood," *The Magazine*, II (March-April, 1935), 230-234;
The Circus in the Attic, and Other Stories, pp. 163-169.

"The Unvexed Isles," *The Circus in the Attic, and Other Stories*, pp. 199-210;
Perspectives USA, No. 13 (Autumn, 1955), 27-37.

"When the Light Gets Green," *Southern Review*, I (Spring, 1936), 799-806;
The Circus in the Attic, and Other Stories, pp. 88-95.

IV. Poems

"Adieu Sentimentale," *Voices*, No. 146 (September-December, 1951), 10.

"Admonition to the Dead," *Double Dealer*, VII (October, 1924), 2;
Fugitives: An Anthology of Verse. New York: Harcourt, Brace & Company, 1928, p. 147.

"Admonition to Those Who Mourn," *Fugitive*, III (December, 1924), 155.

"After Night Flight Son Reaches Bedside of Already Unconscious Father, Whose Right Hand Lifts in a Spasmodic Gesture, as though Trying to Make Contact" (in the sequence entitled "Mortmain"), *Yale Review*, XLIX (Spring, 1960), 393-394. Reprinted (in the same sequence) with the titular addition": 1955" in *You, Emperors, and Others*, pp. 24-25, and in *Selected Poems: New and Old, 1923-1966*, pp. 111-112.

"After Teacups," *Fugitive*, II (August-September, 1923), 106.

"Aged Man Surveys the Past Time" (in a group entitled "Two Poems on Truth"), *American Review*, III (May, 1934), 238-239. Reprinted alone in *Thirty-Six Poems*, p. 43, and in *Selected Poems, 1923-1943*, p. 40.

"Alf Burt, Tenant Farmer," *Fugitive*, III (December, 1924), 154.

"And All That Came Thereafter" (in the sequence entitled "The Day Dr. Knox Did It"), *Encounter*, XXVII (September, 1966), 24. Reprinted in the same sequence in *Selected Poems: New and Old, 1923-1966*, pp. 64-66.

"And Don't Forget Your Corset-Cover, Either" (in the sequence entitled "Ballad of a Sweet Dream of Peace"), *Kenyon Review*, XIX (Winter, 1957), 31-32. Reprinted in the same sequence in the section entitled "Promises" in *Promises: Poems 1954-1956*, pp. 67-68, and in *Selected Poems: New and Old, 1923-1966*, pp. 204-205.

"And Oh—" (in the sequence entitled "Prognosis"), *Sewanee Review*, LXVI (Spring, 1958), 252-254. Reprinted in the sequence entitled "Prognosis: A Short Story, the End of Which You Will Know Soon Enough" in *You, Emperors, and Others*, pp. 58-59.

"Answer Yes or No" (in the sequence entitled "Tale of Time"), *Encounter*, XXVI (March, 1966), 17. Reprinted in the same sequence in *Selected Poems: New and Old, 1923-1966*, p. 23.

"Apology for Domitian" (in the group entitled "Two Pieces after Suetonius"), *Partisan Review*, XXV (Spring, 1958), 223-224. Reprinted in the same group in *You, Emperors, and Others*, pp. 20-21, and in *Selected Poems: New and Old, 1923-1966*, pp. 107-108.

"Arrogant Law" (in the sequence entitled "Garland for You"), *You, Emperors, and Others*, pp. 17-18. Reprinted in the same sequence in *Selected Poems: New and Old, 1923-1966*, p. 106.

"At the hour of the Breaking of the Rocks" (in the sequence entitled "Kentucky Mountain Farm"), *American Caravan.* Edited by Van Wyck Brooks *et al.* New York: The Macaulay Company, 1927, p. 803. Reprinted in the same sequence in the following:

Fugitives: An Anthology of Verse. New York:
Harcourt, Brace & Company, 1928, pp. 139-140;
Vanderbilt Masquerader, X (December, 1933), 16;
Thirty-Six Poems, p. 15;
Selected Poems, 1923-1943, pp. 79-80;
Selected Poems: New and Old, 1923-1966, p. 291.

"Athenian Death," *Nation*, CXLIII (October 31, 1936), 523.

"Aubade for Hope," *American Review*, III (May, 1934), 236-237;
Thirty-Six Poems, p. 47;
Selected Poems, 1923-1943, p. 44.

"August Revival: Crosby Junction," *Sewanee Review*, XXXIII (October, 1925), 439.

"Autumn Twilight Piece," *Double Dealer*, VII (October, 1924), 2.

"Autumnal Equinox on Mediterranean Beach." See "Equinox on Mediterranean Beach."

"Ballad: Between the Box Cars (1923)," *Partisan Review*, XXVII (Winter, 1960), 69-72. Includes the following:
I. ["I Can't Even Remember the Name"],[1] p. 69;
II. ["He Was Formidable"], pp. 70-71;
III. ["He Has Fled"], p. 72.
Reprinted in *You, Emperors, and Others*, pp. 46-50. Includes the following:
1. "I Can't Even Remember the Name," p. 46;
2. "He Was Formidable," pp. 47-48;
3. "He Has Fled," pp. 49-50.
Reprinted in *Selected Poems: New and Old, 1923-1966*, pp. 126-128. Includes the following:
I. "I Can't Even Remember the Name," p. 126;
II. "He Was Formidable," pp. 127-128.

"The Ballad of Billie Potts," *Partisan Review*, XI (Winter, 1944), 56-70;
Selected Poems, 1923-1943, pp. 3-17;
Selected Poems: New and Old, 1923-1966, pp. 223-239.

"Ballad of a Sweet Dream of Peace," *Kenyon Review*, XIX (Winter, 1957), 31-36. Includes the following:
(a) "And Don't Forget Your Corset-Cover, Either," pp. 31-32;
(b) "Keepsakes," pp. 32-33;

[1] Unless otherwise noted, all poem titles appearing in brackets were supplied by the editor from titles subsequently used with a given group of lines.

(c) "Go It, Granny—Go It, Hog!" pp. 33-34;
(d) "Friend of the Family, or Bowling a Sticky Cricket," p. 34;
(e) "You Never Knew Her Either, Though You Thought You Did, Inside Out," pp. 34-35;
(f) "I Guess You Ought to Know Who You Are," p. 35;
(g) "Rumor Unverified Stop Can You Confirm Stop," p. 36.

Reprinted in its entirety in a section entitled "Promises" in *Promises: Poems 1954-1956*, pp. 67-75, and in *Selected Poems: New and Old, 1923-1966*, pp. 204-212.

"Bear Track Plantation: Shortly after Shiloh" (in a group entitled "Two Studies in Idealism: A Short Survey of American, and Human, History"), *Kenyon Review*, XXII (Summer, 1960), 337-338. Reprinted in the same group in *You, Emperors, and Others*, p. 51, and in *Selected Poems: New and Old, 1923-1966*, p. 129.

"Bearded Oaks," *Poetry*, LI (October, 1937), 10-11; *Eleven Poems on the Same Theme*, pp. [2-3]; *Selected Poems, 1923-1943*, pp. 59-60; *Selected Poems: New and Old, 1923-1966*, pp. 273-274.

"Blow, West Wind," *Partisan Review*, XXXIII (Spring, 1966), 220. Reprinted in the sequence entitled "Notes on a Life to be Lived" in *Selected Poems: New and Old, 1923-1966*, p. 5.

"Blue Cuirassier," *Saturday Review of Literature*, VII (July 11, 1931), 953. Reprinted as "The Jay" in the sequence entitled "Kentucky Mountain Farm" in *Thirty-Six Poems*, p. 18, and in *Selected Poems, 1923-1943*, pp. 81-82.

"Boy's Will, Joyful Labor Without Pay, and Harvest Home (1918)," *Botteghe Oscure*, XIX (1957), 203-206. Includes the following:
(a) ["Morning"], pp. 203-204;
(b) ["Work"], p. 204;
(c) ["The Snake"], pp. 204-205;
(d) ["Hands Are Paid"], pp. 205-206.

Reprinted in its entirety in the section entitled "Promises" in

Promises: Poems 1954-1956, pp. 76-81, and in *Selected Poems: New and Old, 1923-1966*, pp. 213-217.

"The Bramble Bush." See "Nursery Rhyme."

["Brightness of Distance"] (in the sequence entitled "Infant Boy at Midcentury," which is in the section called "Promises"), *Encounter*, VIII (May, 1957), 13. Reprinted in the same sequence and section in *Promises: Poems 1954-1956*, pp. 52-53, and in *Selected Poems: New and Old, 1923-1966*, p. 191.

"Brother to Dragons: A Tale in Verse and Voices," *Kenyon Review*, XV (Winter, 1953), 1-103.

The first half of Warren's long poem, *Brother to Dragons;* preprint. Reprinted with the second half in *Brother to Dragons, A Tale in Verse and Voices.*

"Butterflies over the Map" (in the sequence entitled "Mexico is a Foreign Country: Four Studies in Naturalism"), *Poetry*, LXII (June, 1943), 121-122. Reprinted in the same sequence in *Selected Poems, 1923-1943*, p. 51, and in *Selected Poems: New and Old, 1923-1966*, p. 263.

"Calendar," *Thirty-Six Poems*, pp. 57-58;
Selected Poems, 1923-1943, pp. 95-96.

"The Cardinal" (in the sequence entitled "Kentucky Mountain Farm"), *Poetry*, XL (May, 1932), 60. Reprinted in the same sequence in *Thirty-Six Poems*, pp. 17-18, and in *Selected Poems, 1923-1943*, p. 81.

"Chain Saw in Vermont, in Time of Drouth," *Sewanee Review*, LXXIV (Summer, 1966), 590-592. Reprinted as "Chain Saw at Dawn in Vermont in Time of Drouth" in the sequence entitled "Notes on a Life to be Lived" in *Selected Poems: New and Old, 1923-1966*, pp. 15-17.

["The Child Next Door"] (in the sequence entitled "To a Little Girl, One Year Old, in Ruined Fortress"), *Partisan Review*, XXII (Spring, 1955), 172-173. Reprinted in the same sequence in *Promises: Poems 1954-1956*, p. 5, and in *Selected Poems: New and Old, 1923-1966*, p. 149.

"Clearly about You." See "Garland for You: Poem."

"Cold Colloquy," *Thirty-Six Poems*, p. 60; *Selected Poems, 1923-1943*, p. 100.

["Colder Fire"] (in the sequence entitled "To a Little Girl, One Year Old, in Ruined Fortress"), *Partisan Review*, XXII (Spring, 1955), 177-178. Reprinted in the same sequence in *Promises: Poems 1954-1956*, pp. 11-13, and in *Selected Poems: New and Old, 1923-1966*, pp. 155-157.

"Colloquy with Cockroach" (in the sequence entitled "Short Thoughts for Long Nights"), *Botteghe Oscure*, XXIII (1959), 200. Reprinted in the same sequence in *You, Emperors, and Others*, p. 73, and in *Selected Poems: New and Old, 1923-1966*, p. 141.

"Composition in Gold and Red-Gold" (in the sequence entitled "Notes on a Life to be Lived"), *New Yorker*, XLI (February 12, 1966), 30. Reprinted in the same sequence in *Selected Poems: New and Old, 1923-1966*, pp. 6-7.

"Confederate Veteran Tries to Explain the Event" (in the sequence entitled "The Day Dr. Knox Did It"), *Encounter*, XXVII (September, 1966), 23. Reprinted in the same sequence in *Selected Poems: New and Old, 1923-1966*, pp. 61-62.

"Country Burying: 1919" (in the section entitled "Promises"), *Encounter*, VIII (May, 1957), 7-8. Reprinted in the same section in *Promises: Poems 1954-1956*, pp. 32-33, and in *Selected Poems: New and Old, 1923-1966*, pp. 173-174.

"Courtmartial" (in the section entitled "Promises"), *Yale Review*, XLVI (Spring, 1957), 321-325. Reprinted in the same section in *Promises: Poems 1954-1956*, pp. 19-23, and in *Selected Poems: New and Old, 1923-1966*, pp. 160-164.

"Cricket, on Kitchen Floor, Enters History" (in the sequence entitled "Short Thoughts for Long Nights"), *Botteghe Oscure*, XXIII (1959), 201. Reprinted in the same sequence in *You, Emperors, and Others*, p. 77, and in *Selected Poems: New and Old, 1923-1966*, p. 142.

"Crime," *Nation*, CL (May 25, 1940), 655;
Living Age, CCCLIX (January, 1941), 487-488;
Eleven Poems on the Same Theme, pp. [6-7];
Selected Poems, 1923-1943, pp. 25-26;
Selected Poems: New and Old, 1923-1966, pp. 247-248.

"Croesus in Autumn," *New Republic*, LII (November 2, 1927), 290;
Literary Digest, XCV (November 19, 1927), 34;
Fugitives: An Anthology of Verse. New York: Harcourt, Brace & Company, 1928, p. 148;
Brace & Company, 1928, p. 148;
Selected Poems, 1923-1943, p. 89.

"Crusade," *Fugitive*, II (June-July, 1923), 90-91.

"Dark Night Of" (in the section entitled "Promises"), *Encounter*, VIII (May, 1957), 5-7. Reprinted in the same section in *Promises: Poems 1954-1956*, pp. 44-47. Reprinted as "Dark Night of the Soul" in the section entitled "Promises" in *Selected Poems: New and Old, 1923-1966*, pp. 185-188.

"Dark Night of the Soul." See "Dark Night Of."

"Dark Woods" (in the section entitled "Promises"), *Encounter*, VIII (May, 1957), 9-11. Includes the following:
(a) ["Tonight the Woods Are Darkened"], p. 9;
(b) ["The Dogwood"], pp. 9-10;
(c) ["The Hazel Leaf"], pp. 10-11.
Reprinted in its entirety in the same section in *Promises: Poems 1954-1956*, pp. 26-31, and in *Selected Poems: New and Old, 1923-1966*, pp. 167-172.

"Dawn" (in the group entitled "Two Poems about Suddenly and a Rose"), *Saturday Review*, XLIX (August 13, 1966), 21. Reprinted in the same group in the sequence called "Delight" in *Selected Poems: New and Old, 1923-1966*, pp. 87-88.

"Dawn: The Gorgon's Head" (in the sequence entitled "Images on the Tomb"), *Fugitive*, IV (September, 1925), 89. Reprinted in the same sequence in *Fugitives: An Anthology of Verse*. New York: Harcourt, Brace & Company, 1928, p. 143.

"The Day Dr. Knox Did It," *Encounter*, XXVII (September, 1966), 22-24. Includes the following:
1. "Place and Time," p. 22;
2. "The Event," p. 22;
3. "Confederate Veteran Tries to Explain the Event," p. 23;
4. "The Place Where the Boy Pointed," p. 23;
5. "And All That Came Thereafter," p. 24.

Reprinted in its entirety in *Selected Poems: New and Old, 1923-1966*, pp. 58-66.

"Day: Lazarus" (in the sequence entitled "Images on the Tomb"), *Fugitive*, IV (September, 1925), 90. Reprinted in the same sequence in *Fugitives: An Anthology of Verse*. New York: Harcourt, Brace & Company, 1928, pp. 143-144.

"A Dead Language" (in the sequence entitled "Mortmain"), *Yale Review*, XLIX (Spring, 1960), 394-395. Reprinted (in the same sequence) with the titular addition ": Circa 1885" in *You, Emperors, and Others*, pp. 26-27, and in *Selected Poems: New and Old, 1923-1966*, p. 113.

"Death Mask of a Young Man," *Fugitive*, III (June, 1924), 69. Includes the following:
I. "The Mouse," p. 69;
II. "The Moon," p. 69.

"The Death of Isham," *Partisan Review*, XX (July -August, 1953), 393-396. [Excerpt from Warren's long poem, *Brother to Dragons*.]

"Debate: Question, Quarry, Dream," *Yale Review*, XLVII (Summer, 1958), 498-499. Reprinted in the sequence entitled "Some Quiet, Plain Poems" in *You, Emperors, and Others*, pp. 44-45, and in *Selected Poems: New and Old, 1923-1966*, pp. 124-125.

"Deciduous Spring" (in the group entitled "Love: Two Vignettes"), *Saturday Review*, XLIX (August 13, 1966), 21. Reprinted in the same group in the sequence called "Delight" in *Selected Poems: New and Old, 1923-1966*, p. 83.

"Delight." See "Lyrics from 'Delight.' "

["Does the Wild Rose?"] (in the sequence entitled "Homage to Emerson, on a Night Flight to New York"), *New Yorker*, XLII (July 16, 1966), 31. Reprinted in the same sequence in *Selected Poems: New and Old, 1923-1966*, pp. 48-49.

["The Dogwood"] (in the sequence entitled "Dark Woods," which is in the section called "Promises"), *Encounter*, VIII (May, 1957), 9-10. Reprinted in the same sequence and section in *Promises: Poems 1954-1956*, pp. 28-29, and in *Selected Poems: New and Old, 1923-1966*, pp. 169-170.

"Dragon Country: to Jacob Boehme" (in the section entitled "Promises"), *Yale Review*, XLVI (Spring, 1957), 336-338. Reprinted in the same section in *Promises: Poems 1954-1956*, pp. 64-66, and in *Selected Poems: New and Old, 1923-1966*, pp. 202-203.

"Dragon Tree" (in the sequence entitled "Notes on a Life to be Lived"), *New Yorker*, XLI (February 12, 1966), 30. Reprinted in the same sequence in *Selected Poems: New and Old, 1923-1966*, pp. 11-12.

"Dream of a Dream the Small Boy Had," *Saturday Review*, XLIX (August 13, 1966), 21. Reprinted in the sequence entitled "Delight" in *Selected Poems: New and Old, 1923-1966*, p. 86.

"Easter Morning: Crosby Junction," *Fugitive*, IV (June, 1925), 33-34.

"Eidolon," *American Review*, III (May, 1934), 237-238;
Thirty-Six Poems, p. 25;
Selected Poems, 1923-1943, p. 45;
Selected Poems: New and Old, 1923-1966, p. 260.

"Elijah on Mt. Carmel," *New Leader*, XLIII (September 26, 1960), 10. Reprinted in the group entitled "Holy Writ" in *Selected Poems: New and Old, 1923-1966*, pp. 67-68.

"Empire," *This Quarter*, III (July-August-September, 1930), 168-169.

"End of Season," *Nation*, CLIV (March 7, 1942), 286;
Eleven Poems on the Same Theme, pp. [10-11];

Selected Poems, 1923-1943, pp. 37-38;
Perspectives USA, No. 13 (Autumn, 1955), 25-26;
Selected Poems: New and Old, 1923-1966, pp. 256-257.

"Equinox on Mediterranean Beach," *Botteghe Oscure*, XXIII (1959), 203-204. Reprinted as "Autumnal Equinox on Mediterranean Beach" in *You, Emperors, and Others*, pp. 62-63, and in *Selected Poems: New and Old, 1923-1966*, pp. 132-133.

"Evening: The Motors" (in the sequence entitled "Images on the Tomb"), *Fugitive*, IV (September, 1925), 91. Reprinted in the same sequence in *Fugitives: An Anthology of Verse*. New York: Harcourt, Brace & Company, 1928, p. 144.

"The Event" (in the sequence entitled "The Day Dr. Knox Did It"), *Encounter*, XXVII (September, 1966), 22. Reprinted in the same sequence in *Selected Poems: New and Old, 1923-1966*, p. 60.

"Fairy Story," *New Yorker*, XLIII (March 18, 1967), 123.

"Fall Comes in Back-Country Vermont," *New Yorker*, XLI (October 23, 1965), 56-57. Includes the following:
"(1. One Voter Out of Sixteen)," p. 56;
"(2. The Bear and the Last Person to Remember)," p. 56;
"(3. The Human Fabric)," pp. 56-57;
"(4. Afterward)," p. 57.
Reprinted in its entirety in *Selected Poems: New and Old, 1923-1966*, pp. 52-57.

"Fatal Interview: Penthesilea and Achilles." See "Penthesilea and Achilles: Fatal Interview."

"Finisterre" (in the section entitled "Lyrics from 'Delight' "), *New York Review of Books*, [I, No. 1], "Special Issue," 1963, 18. Reprinted in the sequence entitled "Delight" in *Selected Poems: New and Old, 1923-1966*, p. 91.

"The Fierce Horsemen," *Driftwood Flames*. First edition, and popular edition. Nashville: The Poetry Guild, 1923, p. 10.

["The Flower"] (in the sequence entitled "To a Little Girl, One Year Old, in Ruined Fortress"), *Partisan Review*, XXII (Spring,

1955), 173-176. Reprinted in the same sequence in *Promises: Poems 1954-1956*, pp. 6-10, and in *Selected Poems: New and Old, 1923-1966*, pp. 150-154.

"For a Friend Parting," *New Republic*, LXXXI (December 26, 1934), 186. Reprinted as "To a Friend Parting" in the following:
Thirty-Six Poems, p. 45;
Selected Poems, 1923-1943, p. 42;
Selected Poems: New and Old, 1923-1966, p. 259.

"For a Friend Who Thinks Himself Urbane," *Thirty-Six Poems*, p. 63;
Selected Poems, 1923-1943, p. 99.

"For a Self-Possessed Friend," *New Republic*, LXI (November 27, 1929), 14;
Thirty-Six Poems, pp. 61-62;
Selected Poems, 1923-1943, p. 98.

"Foreign Shore, Old Woman, Slaughter of Octopus" (in the section entitled "Promises"), *Yale Review*, XLVI (Spring, 1957), 334-336. Reprinted in the same section in *Promises: Poems 1954-1956*, pp. 42-43, and in *Selected Poems: New and Old, 1923-1966*, pp. 183-184.

"Founding Fathers, 19th Century Style, South-East U. S. A." (in the section entitled "Promises"), *Encounter*, VIII (May, 1957), 11-12. Reprinted in the same section in *Promises: Poems 1954-1956*, pp. 39-41, and in *Selected Poems: New and Old, 1923-1966*, pp. 180-182.

"Fox-Fire" (in the sequence entitled "Mortmain"), *Yale Review*, XLIX (Spring, 1960), 395-396. Reprinted (in the same sequence) with the titular addition ": 1956" in *You, Emperors, and Others*, pp. 28-29, and in *Selected Poems: New and Old, 1923-1966*, pp. 114-115.

"Friend of the Family, Or Bowling a Sticky Cricket" (in the sequence entitled "Ballad of a Sweet Dream of Peace"), *Kenyon Review*, XIX (Winter, 1957), 34. Reprinted in the same sequence in the section entitled "Promises" in *Promises: Poems 1954-1956*, p. 72, and in *Selected Poems: New and Old, 1923-1966*, p. 209.

"The Garden" (in the group entitled "October Poems"), *Poetry*, XLVII (October, 1935), 9-10. Reprinted alone in the following:
Poetry, XLIX (November, 1936), 112;
Thirty-Six Poems, pp. 64-65;
Selected Poems, 1923-1943, pp. 70-71;
Selected Poems: New and Old, 1923-1966, pp. 284-285.

"Garden Waters," *New Republic*, LIV (March 7, 1928), 99;
Thirty-Six Poems, p. 67;
Selected Poems, 1923-1943, p. 101.

"Garland for You," *Virginia Quarterly Review*, XXXV (Spring, 1959), 248-257. Includes the following:

1. "A Real Question Calling for Solution," pp. 248-249;
2. "Lullaby: Exercise in Human Charity and Self-Knowledge," pp. 249-251;
3. "The Letter about Money, Love, or Other Comfort, If Any," pp. 251-255;
4. "The Self That Stares," pp. 255-257.

Reprinted in *You, Emperors, and Others*, pp. 3-19.
Includes the following:

1. "Clearly about You," pp. 3-4;
2. "Lullaby: Exercise in Human Charity and Self-Knowledge," pp. 5-6;
3. "Man in the Street," pp. 7-8;
4. "Switzerland," pp. 9-10;
5. "A Real Question Calling for Solution," pp. 11-12;
6. "The Letter about Money, Love, or Other Comfort, if Any," pp. 13-16;
7. "Arrogant Law," pp. 17-18;
8. "The Self That Stares," p. 19.

Reprinted in *Selected Poems: New and Old, 1923-1966*, pp. 95-106. Includes the following:

I. "Clearly about You," p. 95;
II. "The Letter about Money, Love, or Other Comfort, if Any," pp. 96-99;

III. "Man in the Street," pp. 100-101;
IV. "Switzerland," pp. 102-103;
V. "A Real Question Calling for Solution," pp. 104-105;
VI. "Arrogant Law," p. 106.

"Garland for You: Poem," *Yale Review*, XLVII (Summer, 1958), 494-495. Reprinted as "Clearly about You" in the sequence entitled "Garland for You" in *You, Emperors, and Others*, pp. 3-4, and in *Selected Poems: New and Old, 1923-1966*, p. 95.

"Genealogy." See "Grandfather Gabriel."

"Go It, Granny—Go It, Hog!" (in the sequence entitled "Ballad of a Sweet Dream of Peace"), *Kenyon Review*, XIX (Winter, 1957), 33-34. Reprinted in the same sequence in the section called "Promises" in *Promises: Poems 1954-1956*, p. 71, and in *Selected Poems: New and Old, 1923-1966*, p. 208.

"Gold Glade" (in the section entitled "Promises"), *Encounter*, VIII (May, 1957), 4. Reprinted in the same section in *Promises: Poems 1954-1956*, pp. 24-25, and in *Selected Poems: New and Old, 1923-1966*, pp. 165-166.

"The Golden Hills of Hell," *Driftwood Flames*. First edition, and popular edition. Nashville: The Poetry Guild, 1923, p. 41.

"Goodbye," *American Prefaces*, VI (Winter, 1941), 113-114.

"Grandfather Gabriel," *Second American Caravan*. Edited by Alfred Kreymborg *et al.* New York: The Macaulay Co., 1928, p. 120. Reprinted as "Genealogy" in *Thirty-Six Poems*, p. 28.

"Grasshopper Tries to Break Solipsism" (in the sequence entitled "Short Thoughts for Long Nights"), *Botteghe Oscure*, XXIII (1959), 201. Reprinted in the same sequence in *You, Emperors, and Others*, p. 79, and in *Selected Poems: New and Old, 1923-1966*, p. 143.

["Gull's Cry"] (in the sequence entitled "To a Little Girl, One Year Old, in Ruined Fortress"), *Partisan Review*, XXII (Spring, 1955), 172. Reprinted in the same sequence in *Promises: Poems 1954-1956*, p. 4, and in *Selected Poems: New and Old, 1923-1966*, p. 148.

["Hands Are Paid"] (in the sequence entitled "Boy's Will, Joyful Labor Without Pay, and Harvest Home (1918)"), *Botteghe Oscure*, XIX (1957), 205-206. Reprinted in the same sequence in the section called "Promises" in *Promises: Poems 1954-1956*, pp. 80-81, and in *Selected Poems: New and Old, 1923-1966*, pp. 216-217.

"Harvard '61: Battle Fatigue" (in the group entitled "Two Studies in Idealism: A Short Survey of American, and Human, History"), *Kenyon Review*, XXII (Summer, 1960), 338-339. Reprinted in the same group in *You, Emperors, and Others*, pp. 52-53, and in *Selected Poems: New and Old, 1923-1966*, pp. 130-131.

["The Hazel Leaf"] (in the sequence entitled "Dark Woods," which is in the section called "Promises"), *Encounter*, VIII (May, 1957), 10-11. Reprinted in the same sequence and section in *Promises: Poems 1954-1956*, pp. 30-31, and in *Selected Poems: New and Old, 1923-1966*, pp. 171-172.

["He Has Fled"] (in the sequence entitled "Ballad: Between the Box Cars (1923)"), *Partisan Review*, XXVII (Winter, 1960), 72. Reprinted in the same sequence in *You, Emperors, and Others*, pp. 49-50.

["He passed her only once in a crowded street,"][2] (in the sonnet sequence entitled "Portraits of Three Ladies"), *Double Dealer*, VI (August-September, 1924), 191.

["He Was Formidable"] (in the sequence entitled "Ballad: Between the Box Cars (1923)"), *Partisan Review*, XXVII (Winter, 1960), 70-71. Reprinted in the same sequence in *You, Emperors, and Others*, pp. 47-48, and in *Selected Poems: New and Old, 1923-1966*, pp. 127-128.

["His Smile"] (in the sequence entitled "Homage to Emerson, on a Night Flight to New York"), *New Yorker*, XLII (July 16, 1966), 30. Reprinted in the same sequence in *Selected Poems: New and Old, 1923-1966*, pp. 40-41.

[2] Bracketed title supplied by the editor from the first line of the poem.

"History" (in the group entitled "Two Poems on Time"), *Virginia Quarterly Review*, XI (July, 1935), 353-356. Reprinted alone in the following:
Thirty-Six Poems, pp. 29-33;
Selected Poems, 1923-1943, pp. 30-33;
Selected Poems: New and Old, 1923-1966, pp. 252-255.

"History among the Rocks" (in the sequence entitled "Kentucky Mountain Farm"), *New Republic*, LVII (December 5, 1928), 63. Reprinted in the same sequence in the following:
Vanderbilt Masquerader, X (December, 1933), 16;
Thirty-Six Poems, pp. 16-17;
Selected Poems, 1923-1943, pp. 80-81;
Selected Poems: New and Old, 1923-1966, p. 292.

"Holly and Hickory" (in the sequence entitled "Some Quiet, Plain Poems"), *Saturday Review*, XLI (November 22, 1958), 37. Reprinted in the same sequence in *You, Emperors, and Others*, p. 38, and in *Selected Poems: New and Old, 1923-1966*, p. 120.

"Holy Writ," *Selected Poems: New and Old, 1923-1966*, pp. 67-80. Includes the following:
I. "Elijah on Mount Carmel," pp. 67-68;
II. "Saul at Gilboa," pp. 69-80.

"Homage to Emerson, on a Night Flight to New York," *New Yorker*, XLII (July 16, 1966), 30-31. Includes the following:
I. ["His Smile"], p. 30;
II. ["The Spider"], p. 30;
III. ["One Drunk Allegory"], p. 30;
IV. ["Multiplication Table"], pp. 30-31;
V. ["Wind"], p. 31;
VI. ["Does the Wild Rose?"], p. 31.
Reprinted as "Homage to Emerson, On Night Flight to New York" in *Selected Poems: New and Old, 1923-1966*, pp. 40-49. Includes the following:
I. "His Smile," pp. 40-41;
II. "The Wart," p. 42;
III. "The Spider," p. 43;

IV. "One Drunk Allegory," pp. 44-45;
V. "Multiplication Table," p. 46;
VI. "Wind," p. 47;
VII. "Does the Wild Rose?" pp. 48-49.

"Human Nature" (in the sequence entitled "Short Thoughts for Long Nights"), *Botteghe Oscure*, XXIII (1959), 199.

["I Can't Even Remember the Name"] (in the sequence entitled "Ballad: Between the Box Cars (1923)"), *Partisan Review*, XXVII (Winter, 1960), 69. Reprinted in the same sequence in *You, Emperors, and Others*, p. 46, and in *Selected Poems: New and Old, 1923-1966*, p. 126.

"I Guess You Ought to Know Who You Are" (in the sequence entitled "Ballad of a Sweet Dream of Peace"), *Kenyon Review*, XIX (Winter, 1957), 35. Reprinted in the same sequence in the section called "Promises" in *Promises: Poems 1954-1956*, p. 74, and in *Selected Poems: New and Old, 1923-1966*, p. 211.

["I knew not down what windy nights I fled,"],[3] *Fugitive*, III (April, 1924), 55.

"Images on the Tomb," *Fugitive*, IV (September, 1925), 89-92. Includes the following:
I. "Dawn: The Gorgon's Head," p. 89;
II. "Day: Lazarus," p. 90;
III. "Evening: The Motors," p. 91;
IV. "Night: But a Sultry Wind," p. 92.
Reprinted in its entirety in *Fugitives: An Anthology of Verse*. New York: Harcourt, Brace & Company, 1928, pp. 143-145.

"In Italian They Call the Bird *Civetta*," *Prairie Schooner*, XXXIII (Fall, 1959), 245. Reprinted in the sequence entitled "Some Quiet, Plain Poems" in *You, Emperors, and Others*, pp. 42-43, and in *Selected Poems: New and Old, 1923-1966*, p. 123.

"In Moonlight, Somewhere, They Are Singing" (in the sequence entitled "Some Quiet, Plain Poems"), *Saturday Review*, XLI (November 22, 1958), 37. Reprinted in the same sequence in

[3] Bracketed title supplied by the editor from the first line of the poem.

You, Emperors, and Others, pp. 40-41, and in *Selected Poems: New and Old, 1923-1966*, p. 122.

"In the Turpitude of Time" (in the sequence entitled "Mortmain"), *Yale Review*, XLIX (Spring, 1960), 396-397. Reprinted (in the same sequence) with the titular addition ": N.D." in *You, Emperors, and Others*, pp. 30-31, and in *Selected Poems: New and Old, 1923-1966*, p. 116.

"Infant Boy at Midcentury" (in the section entitled "Promises"), *Encounter*, VIII (May, 1957), 12-13. Includes the following:
(a) ["When the Century Dragged"], p. 12;
(b) ["Modification of Landscape"], pp. 12-13;
(c) ["Brightness of Distance"], p. 13.
Reprinted in its entirety in the same section in *Promises: Poems 1954-1956*, pp. 48-53, and in *Selected Poems: New and Old, 1923-1966*, pp. 189-191.

"Insomnia" (in the sequence entitled "Tale of Time"), *Encounter*, XXVI (March, 1966), 21-23. Reprinted in the same sequence in *Selected Poems: New and Old, 1923-1966*, pp. 34-39.

"The Interim" (in the sequence entitled "Tale of Time"), *Encounter*, XXVI (March, 1966), 18-20. Reprinted in the same sequence in *Selected Poems: New and Old, 1923-1966*, pp. 24-32.

"Into Broad Daylight" (in the section entitled "Lyrics from 'Delight' "), *New York Review of Books*, [I, No. 1], "Special Issue," 1963, 18. Reprinted in the sequence entitled "Delight" in *Selected Poems: New and Old, 1923-1966*, p. 81.

"Intuition" (in a group entitled "Two Poems about Suddenly and a Rose"), *Saturday Review*, XLIX (August 13, 1966), 21. Reprinted in the same group in the sequence entitled "Delight" in *Selected Poems: New and Old, 1923-1966*, p. 89.

"Iron Beach," *Driftwood Flames*. First edition, and popular edition. Nashville: The Poetry Guild, 1923, p. 30. Reprinted without a title in *Fugitive*, III (April, 1924), 54. Reprinted, again as "Iron Beach," in *Fugitive*, IV (March, 1925), 15.

"It Is Not to Be Trusted" (in the section entitled "Lyrics from 'Delight' "), *New York Review of Books*, [I, No. 1], "Special Issue," 1963, 18. Reprinted as "Not to Be Trusted" in the sequence entitled "Delight" in *Selected Poems: New and Old, 1923-1966*, p. 90.

"The Jay." See "Blue Cuirassier."

"Joy" (in the sequence entitled "Short Thoughts for Long Nights"), *Botteghe Oscure*, XXIII (1959), 200. Reprinted in the same sequence in *You, Emperors, and Others*, p. 76.

"Keepsakes" (in the sequence entitled "Ballad of a Sweet Dream of Peace"), *Kenyon Review*, XIX (Winter, 1957), 32-33. Reprinted in the same sequence in the section called "Promises" in *Promises: Poems 1954-1956*, pp. 69-70, and in *Selected Poems: New and Old, 1923-1966*, pp. 206-207.

"Kentucky Mountain Farm,"[4] *American Caravan*. Edited by Van Wyck Brooks *et al.* New York: The Macaulay Company, 1927, p. 803. Is composed of the following:

"At the hour of the Breaking of the Rocks," p. 803.

Reprinted in *Nation*, CXXVI (January 11, 1928), 47. Is composed of the following:

"Rebuke of the Rocks," p. 47.

Reprinted in *Literary Digest*, XCVI (January 28, 1928), 32. Is composed of the following:

"Rebuke of the Rocks," p. 32.

Reprinted in *New Republic*, LVII (December 5, 1928), 63. Is composed of the following:

"History among the Rocks," p. 63.

Reprinted in *Fugitives: An Anthology of Verse*. New York: Harcourt, Brace & Company, 1928, pp. 139-140. Is composed of the following:

I. "Rebuke of the Rocks," p. 139;

II. "At the Hour of the Breaking of the Rocks," pp. 139-140.

[4] The sequence entitled "Kentucky Mountain Farm" includes a number of poems, one or more of which composes the sequence at each printing. as indicated.

Reprinted in *New Republic*, LXI (January 15, 1930), 215. Is composed of the following:
"The Return," p. 215.
Reprinted in *Poetry*, XL (May, 1932), 59-61. Is composed of the following:
"The Owl," pp. 59-60;
"The Cardinal," p. 60;
"Watershed," p. 61.
Reprinted in *Vanderbilt Masquerader*, X (December, 1933), 16. Is composed of the following:
I. "Rebuke of the Rocks," p. 16;
II. "At the Hour of the Breaking of the Rocks," p. 16;
III. "History Among the Rocks," p. 16.
Reprinted in *Thirty-Six Poems*, pp. 14-20. Is composed of the following:
i. "Rebuke of the Rocks," p. 14;
ii. "At the Hour of the Breaking of the Rocks," p. 15;
iii. "History among the Rocks," pp. 16-17;
iv. "The Cardinal, pp. 17-18;
v. "The Jay," p. 18;
vi. "Watershed," p. 19;
vii. "The Return," p. 20.
Reprinted in *Selected Poems, 1923-1943*, pp. 79-83. Is composed of the following:
I. "Rebuke of the Rocks," p. 79;
II. "At the Hour of the Breaking of the Rocks," pp. 79-80;
III. "History among the Rocks," pp. 80-81;
IV. "The Cardinal," p. 81;
V. "The Jay," pp. 81-82;
VI. "Watershed," p. 82;
VII. "The Return," p. 83.
Reprinted in *Selected Poems: New and Old, 1923-1966*, pp. 290-293. Is composed of the following:
I. "Rebuke of the Rocks," p. 290;
II. "At the Hour of the Breaking of the Rocks," p. 291;
III. "History Among the Rocks," p. 292;
IV. "The Return," p. 293.

"Knockety-Knockety-Knock" (in the sequence entitled "Three Nursery Rhymes"), *Yale Review,* XLVII (Summer, 1958), 495-496. Reprinted in the sequence called "Nursery Rhymes" in *You, Emperors, and Others,* pp. 64-65, and in *Selected Poems: New and Old, 1923-1966,* pp. 134-135.

"The Last Metaphor," *New Republic,* LXIX (December 9, 1931), 105;
Thirty-Six Poems, pp. 52-53;
Selected Poems, 1923-1943, pp. 91-92.

"Late Subterfuge," *Thirty-Six Poems,* p. 41;
Selected Poems, 1923-1943, p. 68;
Selected Poems: New and Old, 1923-1966, p. 281.

"The Letter About Money, Love, Or Other Comfort, if Any" (in the sequence entitled "Garland for You"), *Virginia Quarterly Review,* XXXV (Spring, 1959), 251-255. Reprinted in the same sequence in *You, Emperors, and Others,* pp. 13-16, and in *Selected Poems: New and Old, 1923-1966,* pp. 96-99.

"Letter from a Coward to a Hero," *Southern Review,* I (July, 1935), 92-94;
Thirty-Six Poems, pp. 37-40;
Selected Poems, 1923-1943, pp. 27-29;
Selected Poems: New and Old, 1923-1966, pp. 249-251.

"Letter of a Mother," *New Republic,* LIII (January 11, 1928), 212;
Fugitives: An Anthology of Verse. New York: Harcourt, Brace & Company, 1928, pp. 137-138;
Vanderbilt Masquerader, X (December, 1933), 16-17;
Thirty-Six Poems, pp. 26-27;
Selected Poems, 1923-1943, pp. 87-88;
Selected Poems: New and Old, 1923-1966, pp. 297-298.

"Letter to a Friend," *American Review,* III (May, 1934), 236;
Thirty-Six Poems, p. 46;
Selected Poems, 1923-1943, p. 43.

"The Lie," *Poetry,* LXXXII (June, 1953), 125-133. [Excerpt from *Brother to Dragons.*]

"The Limited," *Poetry*, XLI (January, 1933), 200.

"Little Boy Blue" (in the sequence entitled "Three Nursery Rhymes"), *Yale Review*, XLVII (Summer, 1958), 496-497. Reprinted as "News of Unexpected Demise of Little Boy Blue" in the sequence called "Nursery Rhymes" in *You, Emperors, and Others*, pp. 66-67, and in *Selected Poems: New and Old, 1923-1966*, pp. 136-137.

"Little Boy and General Principle" (in the sequence entitled "Short Thoughts for Long Nights"), *Botteghe Oscure*, XXIII (1959), 201. Reprinted in the same sequence in *You, Emperors, and Others*, p. 78.

"Little Boy and Lost Shoe," *New York Review of Books*, VI (February 17, 1966), 23. Reprinted in the sequence entitled "Notes on a Life to be Lived" in *Selected Poems: New and Old, 1923-1966*, p. 8.

"Little Boy on Voyage" (in the sequence entitled "Short Thoughts for Long Nights"), *Botteghe Oscure*, XXIII (1959), 200. Reprinted in the same sequence in *You, Emperors, and Others*, p. 74.

"A Long Spoon" (in the sequence entitled "Short Thoughts for Long Nights"), *Botteghe Oscure*, XXIII (1959), 200.

"Love: Two Vignettes," *Saturday Review*, XLIX (August 13, 1966), 21. Includes the following:

1. "Mediterranean Beach, Day after Storm," p. 21;
2. "Deciduous Spring," p. 21.

Reprinted in its entirety in a sequence entitled "Delight" in *Selected Poems: New and Old, 1923-1966*, pp. 82-83.

"Love's Parable," *Kenyon Review*, II (Spring, 1940), 186-188;
Eleven Poems on the Same Theme, pp. [19-21];
Selected Poems, 1923-1943, pp. 65-67;
Selected Poems: New and Old, 1923-1966, pp. 277-280.

"Lullaby" (in the section entitled "Promises"), *Encounter*, VIII (May, 1957), 13-14. Reprinted as "Lullaby: Smile in Sleep" in the same section in *Promises: Poems 1954-1956*, pp. 54-55, and in *Selected Poems: New and Old, 1923-1966*, pp. 192-193.

"Lullaby: Exercise in Human Charity and Self-Knowledge" (in the sequence entitled "Garland for You"), *Virginia Quarterly Review*, XXXV (Spring, 1959), 249-251.
Reprinted in the same sequence in *You, Emperors, and Others*, pp. 5-6.

"Lullaby: Moonlight Lingers." See "Lullaby in Moonlight."

"Lullaby: A Motion Like Sleep" (in the section entitled "Promises"), *Yale Review*, XLVI (Spring, 1957), 339.
Reprinted in the same section in *Promises: Poems 1954-1956*, pp. 82-83, and in *Selected Poems: New and Old, 1923-1966*, pp. 218-219.

"Lullaby: Smile in Sleep." See "Lullaby."

"Lullaby in Moonlight" (in the section entitled "Promises"), *Yale Review*, XLVI (Spring, 1957), 331-332. Reprinted as "Lullaby: Moonlight Lingers" in the sequence entitled "Man in Moonlight," which is in the section called "Promises," in *Promises: Poems 1954-1956*, pp. 60-61, and in *Selected Poems: New and Old, 1923-1966*, pp. 198-199.

"Lyrics from 'Delight,'" *New York Review of Books*, [I, No. 1], "Special Issue," 1963, 18. Includes the following:
"Into Broad Daylight," p. 18;
"It Is Not to be Trusted," p. 18;
"Something Is Going to Happen," p. 18;
"Finisterre," p. 18.
Reprinted as "Delight" in *Selected Poems: New and Old, 1923-1966*, pp. 81-91. Includes the following:
I. "Into Broad Daylight," p. 81;
II. "Love: Two Vignettes," pp. 82-83;
1. "Mediterranean Beach, Day after Storm," p. 82;
2. "Deciduous Spring," p. 83;
III. "Something Is Going to Happen," pp. 84-85;
IV. "Dream of a Dream the Small Boy Had," p. 86;
V. "Two Poems About Suddenly and a Rose," pp. 87-89;

1. "Dawn," pp. 87-88;
2. "Intuition," p. 89;

VI. "Not to Be Trusted," p. 90;
VII. "Finisterre," p. 91.

"The Mad Druggist" (in the sequence entitled "Tale of Time"), *Encounter*, XXVI (March, 1966), 17. Reprinted in the same sequence in *Selected Poems: New and Old, 1923-1966*, pp. 21-22.

"Mad Young Aristocrat on Beach" (in the section entitled "Promises"), *Yale Review*, XLVI (Spring, 1957), 333-334. Reprinted in the same section in *Promises: Poems 1954-1956*, pp. 62-63, and in *Selected Poems: New and Old, 1923-1966*, pp. 200-201.

"Man Coming of Age" (in the group entitled "October Poems"), *Poetry*, XLVII (October, 1935), 10-11. Reprinted alone in the following:

Thirty-Six Poems, pp. 48-49;
Selected Poems, 1923-1943, p. 69;
Selected Poems: New and Old, 1923-1966, pp. 282-283.

"Man in Moonlight" (in the section entitled "Promises"), *Promises: Poems 1954-1956*, pp. 56-61. Includes the following:

1. "Moonlight Observed from Ruined Fortress," pp. 56-57;
2. "Walk by Moonlight in Small Town," pp. 58-59;
3. "Lullaby: Moonlight Lingers," pp. 60-61.

Reprinted in its entirety in the same section in *Selected Poems: New and Old, 1923-1966*, pp. 194-199.

"Man in the Street" (in the sequence entitled "Garland for You"), *You, Emperors, and Others*, pp. 7-8. Reprinted in the same sequence in *Selected Poems: New and Old, 1923-1966*, pp. 100-101.

"The Mango on the Mango Tree" (in the sequence entitled "Mexico is a Foreign Country: Four Studies in Naturalism"), *Poetry*, LXII (June, 1943), 126-127. Reprinted in the sequence called "Mexico is a Foreign Country: Five Studies in Naturalism" in *Selected Poems, 1923-1943*, pp. 56-57. Reprinted alone in *Perspectives USA*, No. 13 (Autumn, 1955), 22-23. Reprinted in the sequence entitled "Mexico is a Foreign Country: Four Studies in Naturalism" in *Selected Poems: New and Old, 1923-1966*, pp. 269-270.

"Mediterranean Beach, Day after Storm" (in the group entitled "Love: Two Vignettes"), *Saturday Review*, XLIX (August 13, 1966), 21. Reprinted in the same group in the sequence entitled "Delight" in *Selected Poems: New and Old, 1923-1966*, p. 82.

"Mexico is a Foreign Country: Four Studies in Naturalism," *Poetry*, LXII (June, 1943), 121-127. Includes the following:

I. "Butterflies over the Map," pp. 121-122;
II. "The World Comes Galloping: A True Story," pp. 122-123;
III. "Small Soldiers with Drum in Large Landscape," pp. 123-126;
IV. "The Mango on the Mango Tree," pp. 126-127.

Reprinted as "Mexico is a Foreign Country: Five Studies in Naturalism" in *Selected Poems, 1923-1943*, pp. 51-57. Includes the following:

I. "Butterflies over the Map," p. 51;
II. "Siesta Time in Village Plaza by Ruined Bandstand and Banana Tree," pp. 51-52;
III. "The World Comes Galloping: A True Story," p. 53;
IV. "Small Soldiers with Drum in Large Landscape," pp. 54-55;
V. "The Mango on the Mango Tree," pp. 56-57.

Reprinted as "Mexico is a Foreign Country: Four Studies in Naturalism" in *Selected Poems: New and Old, 1923-1966*, pp. 263-270. Includes the following:

I. "Butterflies over the Map," p. 263;
II. "The World Comes Galloping: A True Story," pp. 264-265;
III. "Small Soldiers with Drum in Large Landscape," pp. 266-268;
IV. "The Mango on the Mango Tree," pp. 269-270.

"Midnight," *Fugitive*, II (October, 1923), 142.

"The Mirror," *Fugitive*, IV (March, 1925), 16.

["Modification of Landscape"] (in the sequence entitled "Infant Boy at Midcentury," which is in the section called "Promises"), *Encounter*, VIII (May, 1957), 12-13. Reprinted in the same sequence and section in *Promises: Poems 1954-1956*, pp. 50-51, and in *Selected Poems: New and Old, 1923-1966*, p. 190.

"Monologue at Midnight," *Virginia Quarterly Review*, XII (July, 1936), 395;
Eleven Poems on the Same Theme, p. [1];
Selected Poems, 1923-1943, p. 58;
Selected Poems: New and Old, 1923-1966, pp. 271-272.

"The Moon" (in the group entitled "Death Mask of a Young Man"), *Fugitive*, III (June, 1924), 69.

"Moonlight Observed from Ruined Fortress" (in the section entitled "Promises"), *Yale Review*, XLVI (Spring, 1957), 330-331. Reprinted in the sequence called "Man in Moonlight," which is in the section entitled "Promises," in *Promises: Poems 1954-1956*, pp. 56-57, and in *Selected Poems: New and Old, 1923-1966*, pp. 194-195.

["Morning"] (in the sequence entitled "Boy's Will, Joyful Labor Without Pay, and Harvest Home (1918)"), *Botteghe Oscure*, XIX (1957), 203-204. Reprinted in the same sequence in the section called "Promises" in *Promises: Poems 1954-1956*, p. 76, and in *Selected Poems: New and Old, 1923-1966*, p. 213.

"Mortmain," *Yale Review*, XLIX (Spring, 1960), 393-398. Includes the following:

1. "After Night Flight Son Reaches Bedside of Already Unconscious Father, Whose Right Hand Lifts in a Spasmodic Gesture, as though Trying to Make Contact," pp. 393-394;
2. "A Dead Language," pp. 394-395;
3. "Fox-Fire," pp. 395-396;
4. "In the Turpitude of Time," pp. 396-397;
5. "A Vision: Circa 1880," pp. 397-398.

Reprinted in its entirety (with a few minor revisions in titles) in *You, Emperors, and Others*, pp. 24-33, and in *Selected Poems: New and Old, 1923-1966*, pp. 111-118.

"Mother Makes the Biscuits" (in the sequence entitled "Three Nursery Rhymes"), *Yale Review*, XLVII (Summer, 1958), 497-498. Reprinted in the sequence called "Nursery Rhymes" in *You, Emperors, and Others*, pp. 68-69, and in *Selected Poems: New and Old, 1923-1966*, pp. 138-139.

"The Mouse" (in the group entitled "Death Mask of a Young Man"), *Fugitive*, III (June, 1924), 69.

"Mr. Dodds' Son," *Fugitive*, IV (June, 1925), 35.

["Multiplication Table"] (in the sequence entitled "Homage to Emerson, on a Night Flight to New York"), *New Yorker*, XLII (July 16, 1966), 30-31. Reprinted in the same sequence in *Selected Poems: New and Old, 1923-1966*, p. 46.

"Myth on Mediterranean Beach: Venus Anadyomene as Logos," *Saturday Review*, L (February 25, 1967), 38.

"Necessity for Belief" (in the section entitled "Promises"), *Yale Review*, XLVI (Spring, 1957), 340. Reprinted in the same section in *Promises: Poems 1954-1956*, p. 84.

"News of Unexpected Demise of Little Boy Blue." See "Little Boy Blue."

"Night: But a Sultry Wind" (in the sequence entitled "Images on the Tomb"), *Fugitive*, IV (September, 1925), 92. Reprinted alone in the *Nashville Tennessean*, September 27, 1925, p. 7 ("Firing Line Section"). Reprinted, again in the sequence called "Images on the Tomb," in *Fugitives: An Anthology of Verse*. New York: Harcourt, Brace & Company, 1928, pp. 144-145.

"Nightmare of Man" (in the sequence entitled "Short Thoughts for Long Nights"), *Botteghe Oscure*, XXIII (1959), 199. Reprinted in the same sequence in *You, Emperors, and Others*, p. 72.

"Nightmare of Mouse" (in the sequence entitled "Short Thoughts for Long Nights"), *Botteghe Oscure*, XXIII (1959), 199. Reprinted in the same sequence in *You, Emperors, and Others*, p. 71, and in *Selected Poems: New and Old, 1923-1966*, p. 140.

"Nocturne," *Fugitive*, III (June, 1924), 70.

"Nocturne: Traveling Salesman in Hotel Bedroom," *American Scholar*, XXVIII (Summer, 1959), 306-307;
You, Emperors, and Others, pp. 54-55.

"Not to Be Trusted." See "It Is Not to Be Trusted."

"Notes on a Life to be Lived," *New Yorker*, XLI (February 12, 1966), 30. Includes the following:
I. "Stargazing, p. 30;
II. "Dragon Tree," p. 30;
III. "Composition in Gold and Red-Gold," p. 30.
Reprinted in *Selected Poems: New and Old, 1923-1966*, pp. 3-18. Includes the following:
I. "Stargazing," p. 3;
II. "Small White House," p. 4;
III. "Blow, West Wind," p. 5;
IV. "Composition in Gold and Red-Gold," pp. 6-7;
V. "Little Boy and Lost Shoe," p. 8;
VI. "Patriotic Tour and Postulate of Joy," pp. 9-10;
VII. "Dragon-Tree," pp. 11-12;
VIII. "Vision Under the October Mountain: A Love Poem," pp. 13-14;
IX. "Chain Saw at Dawn in Vermont in Time of Drouth," pp. 15-17;
X. "Ways of Day," p. 18.

"Nursery Rhyme," *Prairie Schooner*, XXXIII (Fall, 1959), 244. Reprinted as "The Bramble Bush" (in the sequence entitled "Nursery Rhymes") in *You, Emperors, and Others*, p. 70.

"Nursery Rhyme: Why Are Your Eyes as Big as Saucers?" *Botteghe Oscure*, XXIII (1959), 201-202.

"Nursery Rhymes." See "Three Nursery Rhymes."

"Obsession" (in the sequence entitled "Short Thoughts for Long Nights"), *Botteghe Oscure*, XXIII (1959), 200. Reprinted in the same sequence in *You, Emperors, and Others*, p. 75.

"October Poems," *Poetry*, XLVII (October, 1935), 9-11. Includes the following:
"The Garden," pp. 9-10;
"Man Coming of Age," pp. 10-11.

["One Drunk Allegory"] (in the sequence entitled "Homage to Emerson, on a Night Flight to New York"), *New Yorker*, XLII (July 16, 1966), 30. Reprinted in the same sequence in *Selected Poems: New and Old, 1923-1966*, pp. 44-45.

"Original Sin: a Short Story," *Kenyon Review*, IV (Spring, 1942), 179-180;
Eleven Poems on the Same Theme, pp. [8-9];
Selected Poems, 1923-1943, pp. 23-24;
Selected Poems: New and Old, 1923-1966, pp. 245-246.

"Ornithology in a World of Flux" (in the sequence entitled "Some Quiet, Plain Poems"), *Saturday Review*, XLI (November 22, 1958), 37. Reprinted in the same sequence in *You, Emperors, and Others*, p. 37, and in *Selected Poems: New and Old, 1923-1966*, p. 119.

"The Owl" (in the sequence entitled "Kentucky Mountain Farm"), *Poetry*, XL (May, 1932), 59-60.

"Pacific Gazer," *Thirty-Six Poems*, pp. 55-56;
Selected Poems, 1923-1943, pp. 93-94.

"Patriotic Tour and Postulate of Joy," *New Yorker*, XLI (January 22, 1966), 28. Reprinted in the sequence entitled "Notes on a Life to be Lived" in *Selected Poems: New and Old, 1923-1966*, pp. 9-10.

"Penthesilea and Achilles: Fatal Interview," *Kenyon Review*, XX (Autumn, 1958), 599-601. Reprinted as "Fatal Interview: Penthesilea and Achilles" in *You, Emperors, and Others*, pp. 34-36.

"Picnic Remembered," *Scribner's Magazine*, XCIX (March, 1936), 185;
Eleven Poems on the Same Theme, pp. [4-5];
Selected Poems, 1923-1943, pp. 61-62;
Selected Poems: New and Old, 1923-1966, pp. 275-276.

"Place and Time" (in the sequence entitled "The Day Dr. Knox Did It"), *Encounter*, XXVII (September, 1966), 22. Reprinted in the same sequence in *Selected Poems: New and Old, 1923-1966*, pp. 58-59.

"The Place Where the Boy Pointed" (in the sequence entitled "The Day Dr. Knox Did It"), *Encounter*, XXVII (September, 1966), 23. Reprinted in the same sequence in *Selected Poems: New and Old, 1923-1966*, p. 63.

"Pondy Woods," *Second American Caravan*. Edited by Alfred Kreymborg *et al.* New York: The Macaulay Co., 1928, pp. 121-122;
Thirty-Six Poems, pp. 21-24;
Selected Poems, 1923-1943, pp. 84-86;
Selected Poems: New and Old, 1923-1966, pp. 294-296.

"Portraits of Three Ladies," *Double Dealer*, VI (August-September, 1924), 191-192. Includes the following sonnets:
I. ["He passed her only once in a crowded street,"],[5] p. 191;
II. ["Since I can neither move you nor the fate
That parts us here, . . ."], p. 191;
III. ["Strangely her heart yet clutched a strange twilight,"], p. 192.

"Praises for Mrs. Dodd," *Fugitive*, III (August, 1924), 118.

"Pro Sua Vita," *New Republic*, L (May 11, 1927), 333;
Fugitives: An Anthology of Verse. New York: Harcourt, Brace & Company, 1928, pp. 149-150

"Problem of Knowledge," *Southwest Review*, XVIII (Summer, 1933), 417;

[5] Bracketed titles in this group supplied by the editor from the first line(s) of the poems.

Thirty-Six Poems, p. 59;
Selected Poems, 1923-1943, p. 97.

"Prognosis," *Sewanee Review*, LXVI (Spring, 1958), 252-255. Includes the following:

I. "And Oh—," pp. 252-254;
II. "What the Sand Said," pp. 254-255;
III. "What the Joree Said," p. 255.

Reprinted as "Prognosis: A Short Story, the End of Which You Will Know Soon Enough" in *You, Emperors, and Others*, pp. 58-61. Includes the following:

1. "And Oh—," pp. 58-59;
2. "What the Sand Said," p. 60;
3. "What the Joree Said, the Joree Being Only a Bird," p. 61.

"Prognosis: A Short Story, the End of Which You Will Know Soon Enough." See "Prognosis."

"Promises," *Yale Review*, XLVI (Spring, 1957), 321-340. Includes the following:

I. "Courtmartial," pp. 321-325;
II. "School Lesson Based on Word of Tragic Death of Entire Gillum Family," pp. 325-328;
III. "Walk by Moonlight in Small Town," pp. 328-330;
IV. "Moonlight Observed from Ruined Fortress," pp. 330-331;
V. "Lullaby in Moonlight," pp. 331-332;
VI. "Mad Young Aristocrat on Beach," pp. 333-334;
VII. "Foreign Shore, Old Woman, Slaughter of Octopus," pp. 334-336;
VIII. "Dragon Country: To Jacob Boehme," pp. 336-338;
IX. "Lullaby: A Motion like Sleep," p. 339;
X. "Necessity for Belief," p. 340.

Reprinted as "Promises": ["To Gabriel (born, July 19th 1955)"] in *Encounter*, VIII (May, 1957), 3-14. Includes the following:

1. "What Was the Promise that Smiled from the Maples at Evening?" pp. 3-4;
2. "Gold Glade," p. 4;

3. "Dark Night Of," pp. 5-7;
4. "Country Burying: 1919," pp. 7-8;
5. "Summer Storm (Circa 1916) and God's Grace," p. 8;
6. "Dark Woods," pp. 9-11;
   (a) ["Tonight the Woods Are Darkened"], p. 9;
   (b) ["The Dogwood"], pp. 9-10;
   (c) ["The Hazel Leaf"], pp. 10-11;
7. "Founding Fathers, 19th Century Style, South-East U. S. A.," pp. 11-12;
8. "Infant Boy at Midcentury," pp. 12-13;
   (a) ["When the Century Dragged"], p. 12;
   (b) ["Modification of Landscape"], pp. 12-13;
   (c) ["Brightness of Distance"], p. 13;
9. "Lullaby," pp. 13-14.

Reprinted as "Promises" in *Promises: Poems 1954-1956*, pp. 17-84, and in *Selected Poems: New and Old, 1923-1966*, pp. 158-219. For a list of the poems included in these sections entitled "Promises," see the table of contents of these two books in Chapter I.

"Pursuit," *Virginia Quarterly Review*, XVIII (Winter, 1942), 57-59;
Eleven Poems on the Same Theme, pp. [14-15];
Selected Poems, 1923-1943, pp. 21-22;
Perspectives USA, No. 13 (Autumn, 1955), 23-25;
Selected Poems: New and Old, 1923-1966, pp. 243-244.

"Question and Answer," *Poetry*, LVII (February, 1941), 288-291;
Eleven Poems on the Same Theme, pp. [16-18];
Selected Poems, 1923-1943, pp. 34-36.

"Ransom," *Southern Review*, I (July, 1935), 95;
Thirty-Six Poems, p. 42;
Selected Poems, 1923-1943, p. 39;
Selected Poems: New and Old, 1923-1966, p. 258.

"A Real Question Calling for Solution" (in the sequence entitled "Garland for You"), *Virginia Quarterly Review*, XXXV (Spring, 1959), 248-249. Reprinted in the same sequence in

You, Emperors, and Others, pp. 11-12, and in *Selected Poems: New and Old, 1923-1966*, pp. 104-105.

"Rebuke of the Rocks" (in the sequence entitled "Kentucky Mountain Farm"), *Nation*, CXXVI (January 11, 1928), 47. Reprinted in the same sequence in the following:
Literary Digest, XCVI (January 28, 1928), 32;
Fugitives: An Anthology of Verse. New York: Harcourt, Brace & Company, 1928, p. 139;
Vanderbilt Masquerader, X (December, 1933), 16;
Thirty-Six Poems, p. 14;
Selected Poems, 1923-1943, p. 79;
Selected Poems: New and Old, 1923-1966, p. 290.

"Resolution" (in the group entitled "Two Poems on Time"), *Virginia Quarterly Review*, XI (July, 1935), 352-353.
Reprinted alone in *Thirty-Six Poems*, pp. 34-36, and in *Selected Poems, 1923-1943*, pp. 63-64.

"The Return" (in the sequence entitled "Kentucky Mountain Farm"), *New Republic*, LXI (January 15, 1930), 215. Reprinted in the same sequence in the following:
Thirty-Six Poems, p. 20;
Selected Poems, 1923-1943, p. 83;
Selected Poems: New and Old, 1923-1966, p. 293.

"The Return: An Elegy," *Poetry*, XLV (November, 1934), 85-89;
Thirty-Six Poems, pp. 9-13;
Selected Poems, 1923-1943, pp. 75-78;
Selected Poems: New and Old, 1923-1966, pp. 286-289.

"Revelation," *Poetry*, LIX (January, 1942), 202-203;
**Angry Penguins* (Australia), September, 1943;
Eleven Poems on the Same Theme, pp. [12-13];
Selected Poems, 1923-1943, pp. 46-47;
Selected Poems: New and Old, 1923-1966, pp. 261-262.

"Rumor Unverified Stop Can You Confirm Stop" (in the sequence entitled "Ballad of a Sweet Dream of Peace"), *Kenyon Review*, XIX (Winter, 1957), 36. Reprinted in the same sequence in the section called "Promises" in *Promises: Poems 1954-1956*, p. 75, and in *Selected Poems: New and Old, 1923-1966*, p. 212.

"Saul," *Yale Review*, LV (Summer, 1966), 481-487. Reprinted as "Saul at Gilboa" in the group entitled "Holy Writ" in *Selected Poems: New and Old, 1923-1966*, pp. 69-80.

"Saul at Gilboa." See "Saul."

"School Lesson Based on Word of Tragic Death of Entire Gillum Family" (in the section entitled "Promises"), *Yale Review*, XLVI (Spring, 1957), 325-328. Reprinted in the same section in *Promises: Poems 1954-1956*, pp. 34-36, and in *Selected Poems: New and Old, 1923-1966*, pp. 175-177.

"The Self that Stares" (in the sequence entitled "Garland for You"), *Virginia Quarterly Review*, XXXV (Spring, 1959), 255-257. Reprinted in the same sequence in *You, Emperors, and Others*, p. 19.

"Shoes in Rain Jungle," *New York Review of Books*, V (November 11, 1965), 10;
Selected Poems: New and Old, 1923-1966, pp. 50-51.

"Short Thoughts for Long Nights," *Botteghe Oscure*, XXIII (1959), 199-201. Includes the following:

I. "Nightmare of Mouse," p. 199;
II. "Nightmare of Man," p. 199;
III. "Human Nature," p. 199;
IV. "Colloquy with Cockroach," p. 200;
V. "Little Boy on Voyage," p. 200;
VI. "Obsession," p. 200;
VII. "A Long Spoon," p. 200;
VIII. "Joy," p. 200;
IX. "Theology," p. 201;
X. "Cricket, on Kitchen Floor, Enters History," p. 201;
XI. "Little Boy and General Principle," p. 201;
XII. "Grasshopper Tries to Break Solipsism," p. 201.

Reprinted in *You, Emperors, and Others*, pp. 71-79. Includes the following:

1. "Nightmare of Mouse," p. 71;
2. "Nightmare of Man," p. 72;
3. "Colloquy with Cockroach," p. 73;
4. "Little Boy on Voyage," p. 74;
5. "Obsession," p. 75;
6. "Joy," p. 76;
7. "Cricket, on Kitchen Floor, Enters History," p. 77;
8. "Little Boy and General Principle," p. 78;
9. "Grasshopper Tries to Break Solipsism," p. 79.

Reprinted in *Selected Poems: New and Old, 1923-1966*, pp. 140-143. Includes the following:

I. "Nightmare of Mouse," p. 140;
II. "Colloquy with Cockroach," p. 141;
III. "Cricket, on Kitchen Floor, Enters History," p. 142;
IV. "Grasshopper Tries to Break Solipsism," p. 143.

"Siesta Time in Village Plaza by Ruined Bandstand and Banana Tree" (in the sequence entitled "Mexico is a Foreign Country: Five Studies in Naturalism"), *Selected Poems, 1923-1943*, pp. 51-52.

["Since I can neither move you nor the fate"][6] (in the sonnet sequence entitled "Portraits of Three Ladies"), *Double Dealer*, VI (August-September, 1924), 191.

["Sirocco"] (in the sequence entitled "To a Little Girl, One Year Old, in Ruined Fortress"), *Partisan Review*, XXII (Spring, 1955), 171. Reprinted in the same sequence in *Promises: Poems 1954-1956*, p. 3, and in *Selected Poems: New and Old, 1923-1966*, p. 147.

"Small Soldiers with Drum in Large Landscape" (in the sequence entitled "Mexico is a Foreign Country: Four Studies in Naturalism"), *Poetry*, LXII (June, 1943), 123-126. Reprinted in the same sequence in *Selected Poems, 1923-1943*, pp. 54-55, and in *Selected Poems: New and Old, 1923-1966*, pp. 266-268.

"Small White House" (in the sequence entitled "Notes on a Life to be Lived"), *Selected Poems: New and Old, 1923-1966*, p. 4.

[6] Bracketed title supplied by the editor from the first line of the poem.

["The Snake"] (in the sequence entitled "Boy's Will, Joyful Labor Without Pay, and Harvest Home (1918)"), *Botteghe Oscure*, XIX (1957), 204-205. Reprinted in the same sequence in the section called "Promises" in *Promises: Poems 1954-1956*, pp. 78-79, and in *Selected Poems: New and Old, 1923-1966*, p. 215.

"So Frost Astounds," *Poetry*, XLIV (July, 1934), 196;
Thirty-Six Poems, p. 51;
Selected Poems, 1923-1943, p. 90.

["So many are the things that she has learned,"],[7] *Fugitive*, III (April, 1924), 54.

"So You Agree with What I Say? Well, What Did I Say?" *You, Emperors, and Others*, pp. 56-57.

"Some Quiet, Plain Poems," *Saturday Review*, XLI (November 22, 1958), 37. Includes the following:

1. "Ornithology in a World of Flux," p. 37;
2. "Holly and Hickory," p. 37;
3. "The Well-House," p. 37;
4. "In Moonlight, Somewhere, They Are Singing," p. 37.

Reprinted as follows in *You, Emperors, and Others*, pp. 37-45, and in *Selected Poems: New and Old, 1923-1966*, pp. 119-125:

1. "Ornithology in a World of Flux";
2. "Holly and Hickory";
3. "The Well House";
4. "In Moonlight, Somewhere, They Are Singing";
5. "In Italian They Call the Bird *Civetta*";
6. "Debate: Question, Quarry, Dream."

"Something Is Going to Happen" (in the section entitled "Lyrics from 'Delight' "), *New York Review of Books*, [I, No. 1], "Special Issue," 1963, 18. Reprinted in the sequence called "Delight" in *Selected Poems: New and Old, 1923-1966*, pp. 84-85.

"Sonnet of August Drouth" (in the group entitled "Sonnets of Two Summers"), *Fugitive*, III (August, 1924), 117.

[7] Bracketed title supplied by the editor from the first line of the poem.

"Sonnet of a Rainy Summer" (in the group entitled "Sonnets of Two Summers"), *Fugitive*, III (August, 1924), 117.

"Sonnets of Two Summers," *Fugitive*, III (August, 1924), 117. Includes the following:
I. "Sonnet of a Rainy Summer," p. 117;
II. "Sonnet of August Drouth," p. 117.

["The Spider"] (in the sequence entitled "Homage to Emerson, on a Night Flight to New York"), *New Yorker*, XLII (July 16, 1966), 30. Reprinted in the same sequence in *Selected Poems: New and Old, 1923-1966*, p. 43.

"Stargazing" (in the sequence entitled "Notes on a Life to be Lived"), *New Yorker*, XLI (February 12, 1966), 30. Reprinted in the same sequence in *Selected Poems: New and Old, 1923-1966*, p. 3.

["Strangely her heart yet clutched a strange twilight,"][8] (in the sonnet sequence entitled "Portraits of Three Ladies"), *Double Dealer*, VI (August-September, 1924), 192.

"Summer Storm (Circa 1916) and God's Grace" (in the section entitled "Promises"), *Encounter*, VIII (May, 1957), 8. Reprinted in the same section in *Promises: Poems 1954-1956*, pp. 37-38, and in *Selected Poems: New and Old, 1923-1966*, pp. 178-179.

"Switzerland," *Kenyon Review*, XX (Autumn, 1958), 602-603. Reprinted in the sequence entitled "Garland for You" in *You, Emperors, and Others*, pp. 9-10, and in *Selected Poems: New and Old, 1923-1966*, pp. 102-103.

"Tale of Time," *Encounter*, XXVI (March, 1966), 16-23. Includes the following:
I. "What Happened," p. 16;
II. "The Mad Druggist," p. 17;
III. "Answer Yes or No," p. 17;
IV. "The Interim," pp. 18-20;
V. "What Were You Thinking, Dear Mother?" pp. 20-21;

[8] Bracketed title supplied by the editor from the first line of the poem.

VI. "Insomnia," pp. 21-23.

Reprinted in its entirety in *Selected Poems: New and Old, 1923-1966*, pp. 19-39.

"Terror," *Poetry*, LVII (February, 1941), 285-288;
Eleven Poems on the Same Theme, pp. [22-24];
Selected Poems, 1923-1943, pp. 18-20;
Selected Poems: New and Old, 1923-1966, pp. 240-242.

"Theology" (in the sequence entitled "Short Thoughts for Long Nights"), *Botteghe Oscure*, XXIII (1959), 201.

"Three Nursery Rhymes," *Yale Review*, XLVII (Summer, 1958), 495-498. Includes the following:
I. "Knockety-Knockety-Knock," pp. 495-496;
II. "Little Boy Blue," pp. 496-497;
III. "Mother Makes the Biscuits," pp. 497-498.

Reprinted as "Nursery Rhymes" in *You, Emperors, and Others*, pp. 64-70. Includes the following:
1. "Knockety-Knockety-Knock," pp. 64-65;
2. "News of Unexpected Demise of Little Boy Blue," pp. 66-67;
3. "Mother Makes the Biscuits," pp. 68-69;
4. "The Bramble Bush," p. 70.

Reprinted, again as "Nursery Rhymes," in *Selected Poems: New and Old, 1923-1966*, pp. 134-139. Includes the following:
I. "Knockety-Knockety-Knock," pp. 134-135;
II. "News of Unexpected Demise of Little Boy Blue," pp. 136-137;
III. "Mother Makes the Biscuits," pp. 138-139.

"Tiberius on Capri" (in the group entitled "Two Pieces after Suetonius"), *Partisan Review*, XXV (Spring, 1958), 224-225. Reprinted in the same group in *You, Emperors, and Others*, pp. 22-23, and in *Selected Poems: New and Old, 1923-1966*, pp. 109-110.

"To Certain Old Masters," *Driftwood Flames*. First edition, and popular edition. Nashville: The Poetry Guild, 1923, pp. 36-37.

"To a Face in the Crowd," *Fugitive*, IV (June, 1925), 36;

Fugitives: An Anthology of Verse. New York: Harcourt, Brace & Company, 1928, pp. 141-142;
Thirty-Six Poems, pp. 68-69;
Selected Poems, 1923-1943, p. 102;
Selected Poems: New and Old, 1923-1966, pp. 299-300.

"To a Friend Parting." See "For a Friend Parting."

"To a Little Girl, One Year Old, in Ruined Fortress," *Partisan Review*, XXII (Spring, 1955), 171-178. Includes the following:
I. ["Sirocco"], p. 171;
II. ["Gull's Cry"], p. 172;
III. ["The Child Next Door"], pp. 172-173;
IV. ["The Flower"], pp. 173-176;
V. ["Colder Fire"], pp. 177-178.
Reprinted in its entirety as "To a Little Girl, One Year Old, in a Ruined Fortress" in *Promises: Poems 1954-1956*, pp. 3-13, and in *Selected Poems: New and Old, 1923-1966*, pp. 147-157.

"To One Awake," *New Republic*, LV (May 30, 1928), 47; *Thirty-Six Poems*, p. 66.

["Tonight the Woods Are Darkened"] (in the sequence entitled "Dark Woods," which is in the section called "Promises"), *Encounter*, VIII (May, 1957), 9. Reprinted in the same sequence and section in *Promises: Poems 1954-1956*, pp. 26-27, and in *Selected Poems: New and Old, 1923-1966*, pp. 167-168.

"Toward Rationality" (in the group entitled "Two Poems on Truth"), *American Review*, III (May, 1934), 239. Reprinted alone in *Thirty-Six Poems*, p. 44, and in *Selected Poems, 1923-1943*, p. 41.

"Tryst on Vinegar Hill," *This Quarter*, II (January-February-March, 1930), 503-504.

"Two Pieces After Suetonius," *Partisan Review*, XXV (Spring, 1958), 223-225. Includes the following:
I. "Apology for Domitian," pp. 223-224;
II. "Tiberius on Capri," pp. 224-225.
Reprinted in its entirety in *You, Emperors, and Others*, pp.

20-23, and in *Selected Poems: New and Old, 1923-1966*, pp. 107-110.

"Two Poems about Suddenly and a Rose," *Saturday Review*, XLIX (August 13, 1966), 21. Includes the following:
1. "Dawn," p. 21;
2. "Intuition," p. 21.
Reprinted in its entirety in the sequence entitled "Delight" in *Selected Poems: New and Old, 1923-1966*, pp. 87-89.

"Two Poems on Time," *Virginia Quarterly Review*, XI (July, 1935), 352-356. Includes the following:
I. "Resolution," pp. 352-353;
II. "History," pp. 353-356.

"Two Poems on Truth," *American Review*, III (May, 1934), 238-239. Includes the following:
I. "Aged Man Surveys the Past Time," pp. 238-239;
II. "Toward Rationality," p. 239.

"Two Studies in Idealism: A Short Survey of American, and Human, History," *Kenyon Review*, XXII (Summer, 1960), 337-339. Includes the following:
1. "Bear Track Plantation: Shortly after Shiloh," pp. 337-338;
2. "Harvard '61: Battle Fatigue," pp. 338-339.
Reprinted in its entirety in *You, Emperors, and Others*, pp. 51-53, and in *Selected Poems: New and Old, 1923-1966*, pp. 129-131.

"Variation: Ode to Fear," *Selected Poems, 1923-1943*, pp. 48-50.

"Vision," *American Poetry Magazine*, V (December, 1922), 23.

"A Vision: Circa 1880" (in the sequence entitled "Mortmain"), *Yale Review*, XLIX (Spring, 1960), 397-398. Reprinted in the same sequence in *You, Emperors, and Others*, pp. 32-33, and in *Selected Poems: New and Old, 1923-1966*, pp. 117-118.

"Vision Under the October Mountain: A Love Poem," *Sewanee Review*, LXXIV (Summer, 1966), 589-590. Reprinted in the sequence entitled "Notes on a Life to be Lived" in *Selected Poems: New and Old, 1923-1966*, pp. 13-14.

"Walk by Moonlight in Small Town" (in the section entitled "Promises"), *Yale Review*, XLVI (Spring, 1957), 328-330. Reprinted in the sequence called "Man in Moonlight," which is in the section entitled "Promises," in *Promises: Poems 1954-1956*, pp. 58-59, and in *Selected Poems: New and Old, 1923-1966*, pp. 196-197.

"The Wart" (in the sequence entitled "Homage to Emerson, On Night Flight to New York"), *Selected Poems: New and Old, 1923-1966*, p. 42.

"Watershed" (in the sequence entitled "Kentucky Mountain Farm"), *Poetry*, XL (May, 1932), 61. Reprinted in the same sequence in *Thirty-Six Poems*, p. 19, and in *Selected Poems, 1923-1943*, p. 82.

"Ways of Day," *Sewanee Review*, LXXIV (Summer, 1966), 592. Reprinted in the sequence entitled "Notes on a Life to be Lived" in *Selected Poems: New and Old, 1923-1966*, p. 18.

"The Well-House" (in the sequence entitled "Some Quiet, Plain Poems"), *Saturday Review*, XLI (November 22, 1958), 37. Reprinted in the same sequence in *You, Emperors, and Others*, p. 39, and in *Selected Poems: New and Old, 1923-1966*, p. 121.

"What Happened" (in the sequence entitled "Tale of Time"), *Encounter*, XXVI (March, 1966), 16. Reprinted in the same sequence in *Selected Poems: New and Old, 1923-1966*, pp. 19-20.

"What the Joree Said" (in the sequence entitled "Prognosis"), *Sewanee Review*, LXVI (Spring, 1958), 255. Reprinted as "What the Joree Said, the Joree Being Only a Bird" in the sequence entitled "Prognosis: A Stort Story, the End of Which You Will Know Soon Enough" in *You, Emperors, and Others*, p. 61.

"What the Joree Said, the Joree Being Only a Bird." See "What the Joree Said."

"What the Sand Said" (in the sequence entitled "Prognosis"), *Sewanee Review*, LXVI (Spring, 1958), 254-255. Reprinted in the sequence called "Prognosis: A Short Story, the End of Which You Will Know Soon Enough" in *You, Emperors, and Others*, p. 60.

"What Was the Promise That Smiled from the Maples at Evening?" (in the section entitled "Promises"), *Encounter*, VIII (May, 1957), 3-4. Reprinted in the same section in *Promises: Poems 1954-1956*, pp. 17-18, and in *Selected Poems: New and Old, 1923-1966*, pp. 158-159.

"What Were You Thinking, Dear Mother?" (in the sequence entitled "Tale of Time"), *Encounter*, XXVI (March, 1966), 20-21. Reprinted in the same sequence in *Selected Poems: New and Old, 1923-1966*, p. 33.

["When the Century Dragged"] (in the sequence entitled "Infant Boy at Midcentury," which is in the section called "Promises"), *Encounter*, VIII (May, 1957), 12. Reprinted in the same sequence and section in *Promises: Poems 1954-1956*, pp. 48-49, and in *Selected Poems: New and Old, 1923-1966*, p. 189.

"Where the Slow Fig," *New Yorker*, XLIII (June 10, 1967), 145.

"Whiteness of Fog on Wintry Mountains," *Reporter*, XXXVII (September 21, 1967), 49.

"Wild Oats," *Driftwood Flames*. First edition, and popular edition. Nashville: The Poetry Guild, 1923, p. 17.

["Wind"] (in the sequence entitled "Homage to Emerson, on a Night Flight to New York"), *New Yorker*, XLII (July 16, 1966), 31. Reprinted in the same sequence in *Selected Poems: New and Old, 1923-1966*, p. 47.

["Work"] (in the sequence entitled "Boy's Will, Joyful Labor Without Pay, and Harvest Home (1918)"), *Botteghe Oscure*, XIX (1957), 204. Reprinted in the same sequence in the section called "Promises" in *Promises: Poems 1954-1956*, p. 77, and in *Selected Poems: New and Old, 1923-1966*, p. 214.

"The World Comes Galloping: A True Story" (in the sequence entitled "Mexico is a Foreign Country: Four Studies in Naturalism"), *Poetry*, LXII (June, 1943), 122-123. Reprinted in the same sequence in *Selected Poems, 1923-1943*, p. 53, and in *Selected Poems: New and Old, 1923-1966*, pp. 264-265.

"The Wrestling Match," *Fugitive*, IV (June, 1925), 37; *Fugitives: An Anthology of Verse*. New York: Harcourt, Brace & Company, 1928, p. 146.

"You Never Knew Her Either, Though You Thought You Did." See "You Never Knew Her Either, Though You Thought You Did, Inside Out."

"You Never Knew Her Either, Though You Thought You Did, Inside Out" (in the sequence entitled "Ballad of a Sweet Dream of Peace"), *Kenyon Review*, XIX (Winter, 1957), 34-35. Reprinted in the same sequence in the section called "Promises" in *Promises: Poems 1954-1956*, p. 73. Reprinted as "You Never Knew Her Either, Though You Thought You Did" in the same sequence and section in *Selected Poems: New and Old, 1923-1966*, p. 210.

V. Essays and Articles

" 'All the King's Men': The Matrix of Experience," *Yale Review*, LIII (Winter, 1964), 161-167. Reprinted in *Robert Penn Warren: A Collection of Critical Essays*. Edited by John Lewis Longley, Jr. New York: New York University Press, 1965, pp. 75-81.

"An American Tragedy," *Yale Review*, LII (Autumn, 1962), 1-15. *Reprinted as "Introduction" in *An American Tragedy*. By Theodore Dreiser. World Publishing Co., 1962.

"Arnold vs. the 19th Century," *Kenyon Review*, I, Spring, 1939), 217-221.

"The Blind Poet: Sidney Lanier," *American Review*, II (November, 1933), 27-45.

"The Briar Patch," *I'll Take My Stand: The South and the Agrarian Tradition*. By Twelve Southerners. New York and London: Harper & Brothers Publishers, 1930, pp. 246-264; New York: Peter Smith, 1951, pp. 246-264; New York: Harper Torchbooks, 1962, pp. 246-264.

"Character Is Action," *Writer*, LXIII (June, 1950), 181. (With Cleanth Brooks.) [Excerpt from *Understanding Fiction*.]

"Courses in Writing," *Yale Literary Magazine*. Reprinted in *Art and the Craftsman: The Best of the Yale Literary Magazine, 1836-1961*. Edited by Joseph Harned and Neil Goodwin. Carbondale: Southern Illinois University Press, 1961, pp. 278-279.

"Cowley's Faulkner," *New Republic*, CXV (August 12, 1946), 176-180; (August 26, 1946), 234-237. [In two installments.] Reprinted as follows:

"William Faulkner," *Forms of Modern Fiction: Essays Collected in Honor of Joseph Warren Beach.* Edited by William Van O'Connor. Minneapolis: The University of Minnesota Press, 1948, pp. 125-143;
"William Faulkner [1946]," *Literary Opinion in America.* Edited by Morton Dauwen Zabel. Revised edition. New York: Harper & Brothers, 1951, pp. 464-477; Third edition, revised. New York: Harper & Row, 1962, Vol. II, pp. 464-477 (Harper Torchbooks);
"William Faulkner," *William Faulkner: Two Decades of Criticism.* Edited by Frederick J. Hoffman and O. W. Vickery. East Lansing: Michigan State College Press, 1951, pp. 82-101;
"William Faulkner [1946]," *Literature in America.* Selected and introduced by Philip Rahv. New York: Meridian Books, 1957, pp. 415-430;
"William Faulkner," *William Faulkner: Three Decades of Criticism.* Edited by Frederick J. Hoffman and Olga W. Vickery. East Lansing: Michigan State University Press, 1960, pp. 109-124.

"Divided South Searches Its Soul," *Life,* XLI (July 9, 1956), pp. 98-99, 101-102, 105-106, 108, 111-112, 114.
Reprinted in *Great Reading from Life: A Treasury of the Best Stories and Articles.* Chosen by the Editors. New York: Harper & Brothers, 1960, pp. 259-273. [Printed as parts of *Segregation: The Inner Conflict in the South.*]

"Dixie Looks at Mrs. Gerould," *American Review,* VI (March, 1936), 585-595. (With Cleanth Brooks.)

"E. E. Cummings: *lxl,*" *Accent,* IV (Summer, 1944), 251-253.

"Editorial," *Southern Review,* VII (Autumn, 1941), iv, vi, viii, x, xii. (Unsigned; presumably by Cleanth Brooks and Warren.) [Concerns an essay by Howard Mumford Jones on literary criticism.]

"Elizabeth Madox Roberts: Life is from Within," *Saturday Review,* XLVI (March 2, 1963), 20-21, 38.

"Ernest Hemingway." See "Hemingway."

"Faulkner: The South and the Negro," *Southern Review*, n. s. I (Summer, 1965), 501-529. Reprinted in revised form as "Faulkner: The South, the Negro, and Time" in *Faulkner: A Collection of Critical Essays*. Edited by Robert Penn Warren. Englewood Cliffs, N. J.: Prentice-Hall, Inc., 1966, pp. 251-271.
"A substantial part of [the article in *Southern Review*] was delivered at the Southern Literary Festival, at the University of Mississippi, April 23, 1965."

"Faulkner: The South, the Negro, and Time." See "Faulkner: The South and the Negro."

"'The Great Mirage': Conrad and *Nostromo*." See "Nostromo."

"The Hamlet of Thomas Wolfe." See "A Note on the Hamlet of Thomas Wolfe."

"Hawthorne, Anderson and Frost," *New Republic*, LIV (May 16, 1928), 399-401.

"Hemingway," *Kenyon Review*, IX (Winter, 1947), 1-28. Reprinted as follows:
"Hemingway," *Die Amerikanische Rundschau*, III (December, 1947), 89-104. (In German.);
"Introduction," *A Farewell to Arms*. By Ernest Hemingway. New York: Charles Scribner's Sons, 1949, pp. vii-xxxvi. (Modern Standard Authors edition.);
"Hemingway [1947]," *Literary Opinion in America*. Edited by Morton Dauwen Zabel. Revised edition. New York: Harper & Brothers, 1951, pp. 444-463; Third edition, revised. New York: Harper & Row, 1962, Vol. II, pp. 444-463 (Harper Torchbooks).
Reprinted in revised and enlarged form as follows:
"Ernest Hemingway," *Critiques and Essays on Modern Fiction, 1920-1951*. Selected by John W. Aldridge. New York: The Ronald Press Company, 1952, pp. 447-473;
"Ernest Hemingway," *Selected Essays*, pp. 80-118.

"Homage to Oliver Allston," *Kenyon Review*, IV (Spring, 1942), 259-263.

"Homage to T. S. Eliot," *Harvard Advocate*, CXXV (December, 1938), 46.

"How Texas Won Her Freedom," *Holiday*, XXIII (March, 1958), 72-73, 160, 162-167.

"An Interpretation of T. S. Eliot's 'The Love Song of J. Alfred Prufrock,'" *The Creative Reader: An Anthology of Fiction, Drama, and Poetry*. By Robert Wooster Stallman and R. E. Watters. New York: The Ronald Press Company, 1954, pp. 878-885. (With Cleanth Brooks.)

"Introduction: Faulkner: Past and Future," *Faulkner: A Collection of Critical Essays*. Edited by Robert Penn Warren. Englewood Cliffs, N. J.: Prentice-Hall, Inc., 1966, pp. 1-22.

"Introduction," *A Long Fourth and Other Stories*. By Peter Taylor. New York: Harcourt, Brace and Company, 1948, pp. vii-x.

"Irony with a Center: Katherine Anne Porter." See "Katherine Anne Porter (Irony with a Center)."

"James Stephens Again," *Poetry*, XL (July, 1932), 229-232.

"Jeffers on the Age," *Poetry*, XLIX (February, 1937), 279-282.

"John Crowe Ransom: Some Random Remarks," *Shenandoah*, XIV (Spring, 1963), 19-21.

"John Crowe Ransom: A Study in Irony," *Virginia Quarterly Review*, XI (January, 1935), 93-112.

"Katherine Anne Porter (Irony with a Center)," *Kenyon Review*, IV (Winter, 1942), 29-42. Reprinted as "Irony with a Center: Katherine Anne Porter" in *Selected Essays*, pp. 136-156.

"The Killers," *American Prefaces*, VII (Spring, 1942), 195-209. (With Cleanth Brooks.)

"Knowledge and the Image of Man," *Sewanee Review*, LXIII (Spring, 1955), 182-192. Reprinted in *Robert Penn Warren: A Collection of Critical Essays*. Edited by John Lewis Longley, Jr. New York: New York University Press, 1965, pp. 237-246.

[A speech made at the conference on the Unity of Knowledge during the Bicentennial celebration of Columbia University in 1954.]

*"Learning to Write," *Descant*, IX (Spring, 1965), 2-11.

"A Lesson Read in American Books," *New York Times Book Review*, LX (December 11, 1955), 1, 33. Reprinted in the following:
"Toward Liberal Education" in *Readings for Liberal Education*. Edited by Louis G. Locke, William M. Gibson, and George Arms. New York: Rinehart & Company, Inc., 1957, pp. 410-413;
Toward Liberal Education. Edited by Louis G. Locke, William M. Gibson, and George Arms. Fourth edition. New York: Holt, Rinehart and Winston, 1962, pp. 389-392.

"Literature as a Symptom." See "Some Recent Novels."

"Love and Separateness in Eudora Welty." See "The Love and the Separateness in Miss Welty."

"The Love and the Separateness in Miss Welty," *Kenyon Review*, VI (Spring, 1944), 246-259. Reprinted as "Love and Separateness in Eudora Welty" in *Selected Essays*, pp. 156-169.

"Malcolm X: Mission and Meaning," *Yale Review*, LVI (Winter, 1967), 161-171.

"A Mark Deep on a Nation's Soul," *Life*, L (March 17, 1961), 82-89. [Adapted from Robert Penn Warren's *The Legacy of the Civil War: Meditations on the Centennial*.]

"Melville the Poet," *Kenyon Review*, VIII (Spring, 1946), 208-223. Reprinted in the following:
Selected Essays, pp. 184-198;
Melville: A Collection of Critical Essays. Edited by Richard Chase. Englewood Cliffs, N. J.: Prentice-Hall, Inc., 1962, pp. 144-155.

"Melville's Poems," *Southern Review*, n. s. III (Autumn, 1967), 799-855.

"Moravia Ban Opposed," *New York Times,* August 3, 1952, sec. 4, p. 8. [A letter to the editor, signed by Warren and other American authors, deploring the State Department's refusal to grant a visa to Alberto Moravia.]

"The Negro Now," *Look,* XXIX (March 23, 1965), 23-31. [Adapted from *Who Speaks for the Negro?*]

"Nostromo," *Sewanee Review,* LIX (Summer, 1951), 363-391. Reprinted as follows:
Introduction to *Nostromo.* By Joseph Conrad. New York: The Modern Library, 1951, pp. vii-xxxix;
" 'The Great Mirage': Conrad and *Nostromo,*" *Selected Essays,* pp. 31-58;
"On *Nostromo,*" *The Art of Joseph Conrad: A Critical Symposium.* Edited by R. W. Stallman. East Lansing: Michigan State University Press, 1960, pp. 209-227.

"Not Local Color," *Virginia Quarterly Review,* VIII (January, 1932), 153-160.

"A Note on the Hamlet of Thomas Wolfe," *American Review,* V (May, 1935), 191-208. Reprinted as follows:
"The Hamlet of Thomas Wolfe," *Literary Opinion in America.* Edited by Morton Dauwen Zabel. New York: Harper & Brothers, 1937, pp. 359-372;
"A Note on the Hamlet of Thomas Wolfe," *Selected Essays,* pp. 170-183.

"A Note on Three Southern Poets," *Poetry,* XL (May, 1932), 103-113. [On Fletcher, Davidson, and Ransom.]

"A Note to *All the King's Men,*" *Sewanee Review,* LXI (Summer, 1953), 476-480. Reprinted in revised form as the introduction to *All the King's Men.* New York: Modern Library, 1953.

"Notes," *Modern Poetry, American and British.* Edited by Kimon Friar and John Malcolm Brinnin. New York: Appleton-Century-Crofts, Inc., 1951, pp. 541-543. [Warren's background and explanatory notes on "Revelation," "Pursuit," and "Terror."]

*"Novelist-Philosopher—X Hemingway," *Horizon*, XV (April, 1947), 156-179.

"On Faulkner's *A Rose for Emily*," "Introduction to Literature" in *Readings for Liberal Education*. Edited by Louis G. Locke, William M. Gibson, and George Arms. New York: Rinehart & Company, 1948, pp. 187-191; Revised edition. New York: Rinehart & Company, 1952, pp. 451-455; Third edition. New York: Rinehart & Company, Inc., 1957, pp. 443-446. (With Cleanth Brooks.) [From *Understanding Fiction* (1943).]

"On *Nostromo*." See "Nostromo."

"On Writing," *The Creative Mind and Method*. Edited by Jack D. Summerfield and Lorlyn Thatcher. Austin: University of Texas Press, 1960, pp. 59-63. [*The Creative Mind and Method* is a supplement to *The Texas Quarterly*, Vol. III, No. ii.]

"Paul Rosenfeld: Prompter of Fiction," *Commonweal*, XLVI (August 15, 1947), 424-426.

"A Poem of Pure Imagination: An Experiment in Reading," *The Rime of the Ancient Mariner*. By Samuel Taylor Coleridge. New York City: Reynal & Hitchcock, 1946, pp. 59-148. Reprinted as follows.

"A Poem of Pure Imagination (Reconsiderations VI)," *Kenyon Review*, VIII (Summer, 1946), 391-427. (This essay is sections III, IV, and V of the longer essay of the same name. "The sections of the study . . . printed [in *Kenyon Review*] were delivered, in substantially their present form, as a lecture on the Bergen Foundation of Yale University.");

"A Poem of Pure Imagination: an Experiment in Reading," *Selected Essays*, pp. 198-305;

"A Poem of Pure Imagination: An Experiment in Reading." Cleveland: Micro Photo, 1962.

This essay, as it appears in *The Rime of the Ancient Mariner*, is reviewed as follows:

Blackmur, R. P. "Uncle! Uncle!" *Nation*, CLXIV (March 15, 1947), 307-309.

Bostetter, Edward E. "The Nightmare World of *The Ancient*

Mariner," *Studies in Romanticism*, I (Summer, 1962), 241-254.

Breit, Harvey. *New York Times Book Review*, January 5, 1947, p. 5.

Burke, Kenneth. "Towards Objective Criticism," *Poetry*, LXX (April, 1947), 42-47.

Griggs, Earl Leslie. "Date Shells and the Eye of the Critic," *Virginia Quarterly Review*, XXIII (Spring, 1947), 299-301.

Olson, Elder. *Modern Philology*, XLV (May, 1948), 275-279. Reprinted as "A Symbolic Reading of the *Ancient Mariner*" in *Critics and Criticism: Ancient and Modern*. Edited by R. S. Crane. Chicago: University of Chicago Press, 1952, pp. 138-144.

"Poems by Kenneth Patchen," *Nation*, CLV (July 4, 1942), 17.

"The Poetry of Mark Van Doren," *Nation*, CLVI (February 6, 1943), 209-211.

"Poets and Scholars," *Nation*, CLV (August 15, 1942), 137.

"Preface," *Selected Poems*. By Denis Devlin. First edition. New York: Holt, Rinehart and Winston, 1963, pp. 9-14. (With Allen Tate.)

"The Present State of Poetry: III. In the United States," *Kenyon Review*, I (Autumn, 1939), 384-398.

"Pure and Impure Poetry," *Kenyon Review*, V (Spring, 1943), 228-254. [Delivered as one of the Mesures Lectures at Princeton University in 1942.] Reprinted in the following:

Criticism: The Foundations of Modern Literary Judgment. Edited by Mark Schorer, Josephine Miles, and Gordon McKenzie. New York: Harcourt, Brace and Company, 1948, pp. 366-378;

Critiques and Essays in Criticism, 1920-1948. Selected by Robert Wooster Stallman. New York: The Ronald Press Company, 1949, pp. 85-104;

The Kenyon Critics: Studies in Modern Literature from the Kenyon Review. Edited by John Crowe Ransom. Cleveland and New York: World Publishing Company, 1951, pp. 17-42;

Essays in Modern Literary Criticism. Edited by Ray B. West, Jr. New York: Rinehart & Company, Inc., 1952, pp. 246-266; *Selected Essays,* pp. 3-31;
Discovering Modern Poetry. By Elizabeth Drew and George Connor. New York: Holt, Rinehart and Winston, 1961, pp. 391-414.

"The Reading of Modern Poetry," *American Review,* VIII (February, 1937), 435-449. (With Cleanth Brooks.) Reprinted in *Purpose,* X (January-March, 1938), 31-41, where the essay is incorrectly ascribed to Allen Tate. [Read at the meeting of the Modern Language Association at Richmond, Virginia, in December, 1936.]

"Remember the Alamo!" *Holiday,* XXIII (February, 1958), 52-55, 106, 108-110, 112-113.

"Robert Penn Warren," "Some Important Fall Authors Speak for Themselves" in *New York Herald Tribune Book Review,* XXX (October 11, 1953), 10. [Autobiographical sketch, with comments on *Brother to Dragons.*]

"Robert Penn Warren," *Wilson Bulletin,* XIII (May, 1939), 652. [Autobiographical sketch.]

"Robert Penn Warren and Ralph Ellison: A Dialogue," *Reporter,* XXXII (March 25, 1965), 42-46, 48. [Excerpt from *Who Speaks for the Negro?*]

"The Situation in American Writing," *Partisan Review,* VI (Fall, 1939), 112-113.

"The Snopes World," *Kenyon Review,* III (Spring, 1941), 253-257.

"Some Don'ts for Literary Regionalists," *American Review,* VIII (December, 1936), 142-150.

"Some Recent Novels," *Southern Review,* I (Winter, 1936), 624-649. [Part I] of "Some Recent Novels" revised and printed as "Literature as a Symptom" in *Who Owns America? A New Declaration of Independence.* Edited by Herbert Agar & Allen

Tate. Boston and New York: Houghton Mifflin Company, 1936, pp. 264-279.

["Statement Concerning Wallace Stevens's *Harmonium*"], *Harvard Advocate*, CXXVII (December, 1940), 32.

"T. S. Stribling: a Paragraph in the History of Critical Realism," *American Review*, II (February, 1934), 463-486. Reprinted in *Literary Opinion in America.* Edited by Morton Dauwen Zabel. New York. Harper & Brothers, 1937, pp. 372-389.

"The Themes of Robert Frost," *Michigan Alumnus Quarterly Review*, LIV (Autumn, 1947), 1-11. [Delivered as the Hopwood Lecture on May 28, 1947.] Reprinted in the following: *The Writer and His Craft*. Edited by Roy W. Cowden. Ann Arbor: University of Michigan Press, 1954, pp. 218-233;
Selected Essays, pp. 118-136.

"Tradition, Moral Confusion, the Negro: Themes in Faulkner's Work," *Bear, Man, and God: Seven Approaches to William Faulkner's The Bear*. Edited by Francis Lee Utley, Lynn Z. Bloom, and Arthur F. Kinney. New York: Random House, 1964, pp. 166-169. [Excerpted and revised from "William Faulkner" in Warren's *Selected Essays.*]

"Twelve Poets," *American Review*, III (May, 1934), 212-227.

"Two for SNCC," *Commentary*, XXXIX (April, 1965), 38-48. [Excerpt from *Who Speaks for the Negro?*]

"Uncorrupted Consciousness: The Stories of Katherine Anne Porter," *Yale Review*, LV (Winter, 1966), 280-290.

"The War and the National Muniments," *Library of Congress Quarterly Journal of Current Acquisitions*, II (November, 1944), 64-75.

"The Way It Was Written [*Brother to Dragons*]," *New York Times Book Review*, LVIII (August 23, 1953), 6, 25.

"Why Do We Read Fiction?" *Saturday Evening Post*, CCXXXV (October 20, 1962), 82-84. Reprinted in installments as follows:

"Why Do We Read Fiction?" *Time and Tide—John O' London's*, XLIV (January 3-9, 1963), 27;
"Why Do We Read Fiction?—2. Readers Who Play a Double Game," *Time and Tide—John O' London's*, XLIV (January 10-16, 1963), 27;
"Why Do We Read Fiction?—3. Awesome Confrontations," *Time and Tide—John O' London's*, XLIV (January 17-23, 1963), 27;
"Why Do We Read Fiction? —4. The Inner Logic of Fiction," *Time and Tide—John O' London's*, XLIV (January 24-30, 1963), 28;
"Why Do We Read Fiction?—5. The Logic of Motivation," *Time and Tide—John O' London's*, XLIV (January 31-February 6, 1963), 27.

"William Faulkner." See "Cowley's Faulkner."

"William Faulkner" [different essay from the one of the same name listed under "Cowley's Faulkner"], *Selected Essays*, pp. 59-79. Reprinted in the following:
American Critical Essays: Twentieth Century. Selected by Harold Beaver. London: Oxford University Press, 1959, pp. 211-233;
Modern American Fiction: Essays in Criticism. Edited by A. Walton Litz. New York: Oxford University Press, 1963, pp. 150-165.

*"William Faulkner and His South," Charlottesville, Va., March 13, 1951. (Mimeographed.)

In his *The Faraway Country: Writers of the Modern South* (Seattle: University of Washington Press, 1963, p. 245), Louis D. Rubin, Jr., notes that this essay was presented as "a speech at the University of Virginia, distributed as 'the First Peters Rushton Seminar in Contemporary Prose and Poetry' and dated March 13, 1951, pp. 1-15. Much of the content of this essay was later included by Warren in the essay on Faulkner in Warren's *Selected Essays*. . . . For students particularly interested in the South, however, the Charlottesville speech, . . . is well worth reading in its original form."

"William Styron," *Book-of-the-Month Club News*, October, 1967, pp. 6-7, 14.

"Working Toward Freedom," *Poetry*, XLIII (March, 1934), 342-346.

"The World of Daniel Boone," *Holiday*, XXXIV (December, 1963), 162, 164, 166-167, 169-174, 176-177.

"Writer at Work: How a Story Was Born and How, Bit by Bit, It Grew," *New York Times Book Review*, LXIV (March 1, 1959), 4-5, 36. Reprinted in *Opinions and Perspectives*. Edited by Francis Brown. Boston: Houghton Mifflin Company, 1964, pp. 307-313. Reprinted in a somewhat different version as " 'Blackberry Winter': A Recollection" in *Understanding Fiction*. Second edition.

VI. Book Reviews

Abercrombie, Lascelles. *The Poems of Lascelles Abercrombie, Poetry*, XL (April, 1932), 47-50.

Auden, W. H. *The Orators, American Review*, III (May, 1934), 221-224.

———. *Poems* (Second Edition with New Poems), *American Review*, III (May, 1934), 224-227.

Auslander, Joseph. *Sunrise Trumpets, Fugitive*, IV (March, 1925), 29-30.

Bacon, Leonard. *Guinea-Fowl and Other Poultry, New Republic*, LIV (May 2, 1928), 330-331.

Beale, Howard K. *The Critical Year, Virginia Quarterly Review*, VII (April, 1931), 282-287.

Bellow, Saul. *The Adventures of Augie March, New Republic*, CXXIX (November 2, 1953), 22-23.

Bishop, John Peale. *Many Thousands Gone, New Republic*, LXVII (August 5, 1931), 321.

———. *Now With His Love, Poetry*, XLIII (March, 1934), 342-346.

———. *Now With His Love, American Review*, III (May, 1934), 219-221. [Similar to the above review, but not identical.]

Blunden, Edmund. *Halfway House, Poetry*, XLIII (February, 1934), 287-290.

Bradford, Roark. *John Henry, Virginia Quarterly Review*, VIII (January, 1932), 159-160.

Brooks, Van Wyck. *The Opinions of Oliver Allston*, *Kenyon Review*, IV (Spring, 1942), 259-263.

Brown, Harry. *A Walk in the Sun*, *American Scholar*, XIV (Winter, 1944-45), 118-119.

Campbell, Roy. *The Flaming Terrapin*, *Voices*, IV (January, 1925), 89-90.

Chase, Cleveland B. *Sherwood Anderson*, *New Republic*, LIV (May 16, 1928), 400.

Chinard, Gilbert. *Thomas Jefferson: The Apostle of Americanism*, *New Republic*, LXII (April 2, 1930), 196-197.

Chubb, Thomas C. *Ships and Lovers*, *Poetry*, XLII (August, 1933), 292-294.

Coffin, R. P. T. *Ballads of Square-toed Americans*, *Poetry*, XLIV (September, 1934), 334-336.

———. *Red Sky in the Morning*, *Southern Review*, I (Winter, 1936), 637-638.

———. *The Yoke of Thunder*, *Poetry*, XLIV (September, 1934), 336-337.

Coleman, Lonnie. *Escape the Thunder*, *American Scholar*, XIV (Winter, 1944-45), 120.

Colony, Horatio, *Free Forester*, *Southern Review*, I (Winter, 1936), 642.

Cowley, Malcolm (ed.). *The Portable Faulkner*, *New Republic*, CXV (August 12, 1946), 176-180; (August 26, 1946), 234-237. [Review is presented in two installments.]

Cummings, E. E. *lxl*, *Accent*, IV (Summer, 1944), 251-253.

Cutting, Elisabeth. *Jefferson Davis: Political Soldier*, *New Republic*, LXVI (March 25, 1931), 158-159.

Davis, H. L. *Honey in the Horn*, *Southern Review*, I (Winter, 1936), 639-641.

De Capite, Michael. *No Bright Banner*, *American Scholar*, XIV (Winter, 1944-45), 120-121.

de la Mare, Walter. *The Fleeting and Other Poems*, *American Review*, III (May, 1934), 221.

Douglas, Donald. *The Grand Inquisitor*, *Nashville Tennessean*, April 12, 1925, p. 8 ("Firing Line Section").

Dunsany, Lord. *Guerrilla*, *American Scholar*, XIV (Winter, 1944-45), 122.

E., A. *Voices of the Stones*, *Nashville Tennessean*, January 3, 1926, p. 6 ("Firing Line Section").

Ellison, Ralph. *Shadow and Act*, *Commentary*, XXXIX (May, 1965), 91-96.

Fagin, N. Bryllion. *The Phenomenon of Sherwood Anderson: A Study in American Life and Letters*, *New Republic*, LIV (May 16, 1928), 401.

Farmer, James. *Freedom When? New York Review of Books*, VII (August 18, 1966), 22-25.

Fast, Howard. *Freedom Road*, *American Scholar*, XIV (Winter, 1944-45), 117-118.

Faulkner, William. *A Green Bough*, *American Review*, III (May, 1934), 218-219.

______. *The Hamlet*, *Kenyon Review*, III (Spring, 1941), 253-257.

______. *Requiem for a Nun*, *New York Times Book Review*, LVI (September 30, 1951), 1, 31.

______. *These Thirteen*, *Virginia Quarterly Review*, VIII (January, 1932), 160.

Feuchtwanger, Lion. *Simone*, *American Scholar*, XIV (Winter, 1944-45), 122.

Fitzgerald, F. Scott. *The Great Gatsby*, *Nashville Tennessean*, May 24, 1925, [no page given].

Fort, John. *God in the Straw Pen*, *Virginia Quarterly Review*, VIII (January, 1932), 157-158.

Gordon, Caroline. *Aleck Maury, Sportsman*, *Southwest Review* [Book Supplement], XX (January, 1935), 5-10.

———. *Penhally*, *Virginia Quarterly Review*, VIII (January, 1932), 156-157.

Gorman, Herbert. *Nathaniel Hawthorne: A Study in Solitude*, *New Republic*, LIV (May 16, 1928), 399-400.

Green, Paul. *This Body the Earth*, *Southern Review*, I (Winter, 1936), 642-645.

Handlin, Oscar. *Fire-Bell in the Night*, *New York Review of Books*, III (October 22, 1964), 8, 10.

Havighurst, Walter. *Pier 17*, *Southern Review*, I (Winter, 1936), 646-647.

Hays, H. R. *Lie Down in Darkness*, *American Scholar*, XIV (Winter, 1944-45), 119-120.

Hentoff, Nat. *The New Equality*, *New York Review of Books*, III (October 8, 1964), 7-9.

Hillyer, Robert. *Collected Poems*, *American Review*, III (May, 1934), 221.

Humphries, Rolfe. *Out of the Jewel*, *Nation*, CLIV (April 11, 1942), 438-439.

Huxley, Aldous. *Time Must Have a Stop*, *American Scholar*, XIV (Winter, 1944-45), 121-122.

Jeffers, Robinson. *Give Your Heart to the Hawks*, *American Review*, III (May, 1934), 221.

———. *Solstice and Other Poems*, *Poetry*, XLIX (February, 1937), 279-282.

Jones, Madison. *The Innocent*, *Sewanee Review*, LXV (Spring, 1957), 347-352.

King, Martin Luther. *Why We Can't Wait*, *New York Review of Books*, III (October 8, 1964), 7-9.

Lanham, Edwin. *The Wind Blew West*, *Southern Review*, I (Winter, 1936), 642.

Long, Haniel. *Atlantides*, *Poetry*, XLV (January, 1935), 226-228.

Lubell, Samuel. *White and Black: Test of a Nation*, *New York Review of Books*, III (October 8, 1964), 7-9.

Lumpkin, Grace. *A Sign for Cain*, *Southern Review*, I (Winter, 1936), 645-647.

MacLeish, Archibald. *Poems 1924-1933*, *American Review*, III (May, 1934), 212-218.

McCarthy, Mary. *The Company She Keeps*, *Partisan Review*, IX (November-December, 1942), 537-540.

Masefield, John. *A Tale of Troy*, *American Review*, III (May, 1934), 221.

Meadowcroft, Clara Platt. *A Wind Blowing Over*, *Nashville Tennessean*, July 26, 1925, [no page given].

Melville, Herman. *Selected Poems of Herman Melville*. Edited by F. O. Matthiessen. *Kenyon Review*, VIII (Spring, 1946), 208-223.

Milton, George F. *The Age of Hate*, *Virginia Quarterly Review*, VII (April, 1931), 287-288.

Moore, Merrill. *The Noise That Time Makes*, *New Republic*, LXI (January 29, 1930), 280.

Munson, Gorham B. *Robert Frost: A Study in Sensibility and Common Sense*, *New Republic*, LIV (May 16, 1928), 400.

Oskison, John M. *Brothers Three*, *Southern Review*, I (Winter, 1936), 638-639.

Patchen, Kenneth. *The Dark Kingdom*, *Nation*, CLV (July 4, 1942), 17.

Pennell, Joseph Stanley. *The History of Rome Hanks*, *American Scholar*, XIV (Winter, 1944-45), 115-117.

Porter, Alan. *The Signature of Pain and Other Poems*, *New Republic*, LXX (February 24, 1932), 51.

Porter, Katherine Anne. *The Collected Stories of Katherine Anne Porter*, *Yale Review*, LV (Winter, 1966), 280-290.

Pudney, John. *Spring Encounter*, *American Review*, III (May, 1934), 227.

Ramsey, Robert. *Fire in Summer*, *Nation*, CLIV (February 28, 1942), 261-262.

Ransom, John Crowe. *Chills and Fever*, *Voices*, IV (November, 1924), 24-25.

Rawlings, Marjorie Kinnan. *Golden Apples*, *Southern Review*, I (Winter, 1936), 635-637.

Rice, Cale Young. *High Perils*, *Poetry*, XLII (September, 1933), 342-345.

Roberts, Elizabeth Madox. *A Buried Treasure*, *Virginia Quarterly Review*, VIII (January, 1932), 154-156.

Robinson, E. A. *Nicodemus*, *American Review*, III (May, 1934), 221.

———. *Talifer*, *American Review*, III (May, 1934), 221.

Sackville-West, Victoria. *Collected Poems*, *Poetry*, XLVI (September, 1935), 346-349.

Schneider, Isidor. *From the Kingdom of Necessity*, *Southern Review*, I (Winter, 1936), 647-648.

Scott, Evelyn. *A Calendar of Sin*, *Virginia Quarterly Review*, VIII (January, 1932), 158-159.

Silberman, Charles E. *Crisis in Black and White*, *New York Review of Books*, III (October 8, 1964), 7-9.

Sinclair, Upton. *Presidential Agent*, *American Scholar*, XIV (Winter, 1944-45), 122.

Sitwell, Edith. *Rustic Elegies, New Republic*, LIII (November 23, 1927), 23-24.

Sitwell, Sacheverell. *Cyder Feast and Other Poems, New Republic*, LIV (February 29, 1928), 76.

Snaith, J. C. *Thus Far, Nashville Tennessean*, August 9, 1925, p. 6 ("Firing Line Section").

Starke, Aubrey Harrison. *Sidney Lanier, A Biography and Critical Study, American Review*, II (November, 1933), 27-45.

Spender, Stephen. *Poems, American Review*, III (May, 1934), 227.

Stephens, James. *Strict Joy and Other Poems, Poetry*, XL (July, 1932), 229-232.

Stringfellow, William. *My People Is the Enemy, New York Review of Books*, III (October 22, 1964), 8, 10.

Tate, Allen (ed.). *Princeton Verse Between Two Wars: An Anthology, Nation*, CLV (August 15, 1942), 137.

Thomas, Lowell. *Count Luckner, the Sea Devil, New Republic*, LVI (September 5, 1928), 81.

Trilling, Lionel. *Matthew Arnold, Kenyon Review*, I (Spring, 1939), 217-221.

Uhse, Bodo. *Lieutenant Bertram, American Scholar*, XIV (Winter, 1944-45), 122.

Van Doren, Mark. *Our Lady Peace and Other War Poems, Nation*, CLVI (February 6, 1943), 209-211.

Vittorini, Elio. *In Sicily, Nation*, CLXIX (December 3, 1949), 547-548.

Walton, Eda Lou. *Jane Matthew and Other Poems, New Republic*, LXX (February 24, 1932), 51-52.

Weiskopf, F. C. *The Firing Squad, American Scholar*, XIV (Winter, 1944-45), 122.

Welty, Eudora. *The Wide Net*, *Kenyon Review*, VI (Spring, 1944), 246-259.

Werfel, Franz. *The Song of Bernadette*, *Nation*, CLIV (May 30, 1942), 635-636.

Wheelock, John Hall. *The Bright Doom*, *New Republic*, LIV (April 4, 1928), 227.

Wight, Frederick. *South*, *Southern Review*, I (Winter, 1936), 648-649.

Wilson, Edmund. *Note Books of Night*, *Nation*, CLV (December 5, 1942), 625.

———. *Patriotic Gore*, *Commentary*, XXXIV (August, 1962), 151-158.

——— (ed.). *The Shock of Recognition*, *New York Times Book Review*, June 13, 1943, pp. 5, 18.

Winslow, Ann (ed.). *Trial Balances*, *Poetry*, XLVIII (June, 1936), 172-175.

Winston, Robert W. *High Stakes and Hair Trigger: The Life of Jefferson Davis*, *New Republic*, LXVI (March 25, 1931), 158-159.

Wolfe, Thomas. *Of Time and the River*, *American Review*, V (May, 1935), 191-208. Reprinted in the following:
Literary Opinion in America. Edited by Morton Dauwen Zabel. York: Harper & Brothers, 1937, pp. 359-372;
New Selected Essays, pp. 170-183.

Young, Whitney. *To Be Equal*, *New York Review of Books*, III (October 8, 1964), 7-9.

VII. Miscellanea

UNPUBLISHED PLAYS; TELEVISION SERIAL; MOVIES; AND PHONOGRAPH RECORD BY WARREN

Plays

Brother to Dragons. Unpublished play in four acts; based on *Brother to Dragons: A Tale in Verse and Voices.* Copyrighted on April 10, 1957.

Proud Flesh. Unpublished play, 1939.

The Wedding Ring. Unpublished play in three acts. Copyrighted on July 24, 1951.

The Wedding Ring. Unpublished play in two acts; revised from earlier version. Copyrighted on December 27, 1955.

Willie Stark: His Rise and Fall. Unpublished play in three acts; based on *All the King's Men.* Copyrighted on October 17, 1955.

Television Serial

This Very Spot. A dramatic television series by Robert Penn Warren and David M. Clay; script 1: "The Conway Cabal." Copyrighted on December 15, 1952.

Movies[1]

All the King's Men. Columbia Pictures Corporation, 1950; based on the novel of the same name. Copyrighted on January 5, 1950. (Released by Screen Gems, 1954.)

Band of Angels. Warner Brothers Pictures; based on the novel of the same name. Copyrighted on August, 3, 1957.

[1] Scripts not written by Warren.

Phonograph Record

Robert Penn Warren Reading His Own Poems. Phonodisc. Library of Congress, Recording Laboratory album P4 (record P17), 1949. (78 rpm.)

Recorded at the Library of Congress in 1944. Contains two leaflets of bio-bibliographical notes. Poems recorded: "Terror," "Pursuit."

PERIODICALS EDITED BY WARREN

The Fugitive. 4 volumes, April, 1922-December, 1925. Nashville: Fugitive Publishing Company.

Warren and John Crowe Ransom edited Vol. IV, Nos. 1-4 (1925).

Kenyon Review.

Warren served as an advisory editor from Autumn, 1942-Winter, 1963 (Vol. IV, No. 3-Vol. XXV, No. 1).

"Seven Southern Poets," *New Republic,* LXXXI (December 26, 1934), 184-186.

A short anthology of poems, edited by Warren.

Southern Review. 7 volumes, July, 1935-Spring, 1942. Baton Rouge, La.: Louisiana State University Press.

Warren and Cleanth Brooks served as managing editors from 1935 to 1940 (Vols. I-V). Warren, Brooks, and Charles W. Pipkin edited Vol. VI (1940-1941); Warren and Brooks edited Vol. VII (1941-1942).

Southwest Review. Dallas, Texas: Southern Methodist University and Louisiana State University.

Warren served as contributing editor of Vol. XX, No. 1, and as associate editor of Vol. XX, Nos. 2-4. (Vol. XX was published in 1934-1935.)

U. S. Library of Congress Quarterly Journal of Current Acquisitions.

Warren edited Vol. II, Nos. 1-4 (July, 1944-June, 1945).

University of Minnesota Pamphlets on American Writers.

Warren, William Van O'Connor, and Allen Tate are serving as advisory editors of the series.

OTHER MATERIAL BY WARREN

Minard, Michel J. *Ernest Hemingway*. Paris: Lettres Modernes, 1958. ("Avec la collaboration de Robert Penn Warren, *et al.*")

Teacher's Manual to Accompany *Understanding Poetry: An Anthology for College Students*. By Cleanth Brooks and Robert Penn Warren. Revised edition. New York: Henry Holt and Co., Inc., 1951.

VIII. Biographical and Critical Material

BOOKS AND ESSAYS IN COLLECTIONS

Aldridge, John W. *In Search of Heresy*. New York: McGraw-Hill Book Company, Inc., 1956, pp. 73-75 *et passim.*

Concludes that Warren, Allen Tate, and T. S. Eliot embrace "the heresy of literary manners," *i.e.*, they insist "on the need for . . . restraining and defining forms, structures, rituals, patterns, and conventions of conduct. . . ." Alludes to *All the King's Men* in chapters four and five.

All the King's Men: A Symposium. Carnegie Series in English—Number Three. Pittsburgh: Carnegie Institute of Technology, 1957. Includes the following:

Cottrell, Beekman W. "Cass Mastern and the Awful Responsibility of Time," pp. 39-49;

Hart, John A. "Some Major Images in *All the King's Men,*" pp. 63-74;

Schutte, William M. "The Dramatic Versions of the Willie Stark Story," pp. 75-90;

Slack, Robert C. "The Telemachus Theme," pp. 29-38;

Sochatoff, A. Fred. "Some Treatments of the Huey Long Theme," pp. 3-15;

Steinberg, Erwin R. "The Enigma of Willie Stark," pp. 17-28;

Woodruff, Neal, Jr. "The Technique of *All the King's Men,*" pp. 51-62.

Americana Annual 1959. New York: Americana Corporation, 1959, p. 820.

Biographical sketch of Warren.

Anderson, Sherwood. *Sherwood Anderson's Memoirs.* New York: Harcourt, Brace and Company, 1942, pp. 458-459.

Includes Anderson's reminiscences about the Agrarians, and about *We Take Our Stand* [*sic*].

Arms, George, and Kuntz, Joseph M. *Poetry Explication.* The Swallow Press and William Morrow & Company, Inc., 1950, pp. 156-157; Revised edition. By Joseph M. Kuntz. Denver: Alan Swallow, 1962, pp. 276-279.

Contains a checklist of interpretations from 1925 to 1959. (1950 edition checklist extends from 1925 to 1949, and is included in 1962 edition checklist.)

Baumbach, Jonathan. "The Metaphysics of Demagoguery: *All the King's Men* by Robert Penn Warren," *The Landscape of Nightmare: Studies in the Contemporary American Novel.* By Jonathan Baumbach. New York: New York University Press, 1965, pp. 16-34.

Beardsley, Monroe, Daniel, Robert, and Leggett, Glenn. *Theme and Form: An Introduction to Literature.* Englewood Cliffs, N. J.: Prentice-Hall, Inc., 1956, pp. 691-695.

Analyzes the following elements of a short story with reference to Warren's "Blackberry Winter": plot, characters, setting, point of view, attitude and tone, and theme.

Beatty, Richmond C. "The Poetry and Novels of Robert Penn Warren," *Vanderbilt Studies in the Humanities.* Vol. I. Edited by Richmond C. Beatty, J. Philip Hyatt, and Monroe K. Spears. Nashville: Vanderbilt University Press, 1951, pp. 142-160.

Beebe, Maurice, and Field, L. A. (eds.) *Robert Penn Warren's All the King's Men: A Critical Handbook.* Belmont, Calif.: Wadsworth Publishing Company, Inc., 1966.

Available in paperback and text editions.

Bohner, Charles H. *Robert Penn Warren.* New York: Twayne Publishers, Inc., 1964.

Bohner's study of Warren provides "an overview of Warren's literary career, an analysis of the themes which have preoccupied him, and an account of the development of his art as it has deepened and matured." Contains a highly selective bibliography.

Bradbury, John M. *The Fugitives: A Critical Account.* Chapel Hill: University of North Carolina Press, 1958, pp. 172-255, 283-287, *et passim.*

Contains three chapters on Warren: (1) "Warren as Poet," (2) "Warren's Fiction," (3) "Brooks and Warren, Critics." See index for numerous other references to Warren. Also contains a selected bibliography of works by and about Warren.

———. *Renaissance in the South: A Critical History of the Literature, 1920-1960.* Chapel Hill: University of North Carolina Press, 1963, pp. 31-32, 67-70, *et passim.*

Includes critical comments on Warren's poetry and fiction. See index for many scattered references to Warren.

Braithwaite, William S. "Introduction," *Anthology of Magazine Verse for 1925.* Edited by William S. Braithwaite. Boston: B. J. Brimmer Company, 1925, p. xii.

Characterizes *The Fugitive* as "the most distinctive poetry magazine in America."

Brantley, Frederick. "The Achievement of Robert Penn Warren," *Modern American Poetry.* Edited by B. Rajan. New York: Roy Publishers, 1952, pp. 66-80.

Brooks, Cleanth. *The Hidden God: Studies in Hemingway, Faulkner, Yeats, Eliot, and Warren.* New Haven and London: Yale University Press, 1963, pp. 98-127 *et passim.*

Brooks examines Warren's themes and philosophy in a chapter entitled "R. P. Warren: Experience Redeemed in Knowledge."

———. *Modern Poetry and the Tradition.* Chapel Hill: University of North Carolina Press, 1939, pp. x, 74, 77-87; New York: Oxford University Press, 1965, pp. xxiii-xxv, 77-87.

Both editions discuss several aspects of Warren's poetry: structure, theme, tone, rhythm, and imagery. Later edition offers a critical estimate of Warren's poetry in the "Retrospective Introduction."

———. "Warren's Bearded Oaks," *Reading Modern Poetry*. By Paul Engle and Warren Carrier. Chicago: Scott, Foresman and Company, 1955, pp. 106-108.

An explication and criticism of "Bearded Oaks"; from Brooks's *Modern Poetry and the Tradition.*

———. *The Well Wrought Urn.* New York: Harcourt, Brace & World Inc., 1947, pp. 42, 212.

Includes observations by Warren on Shakespeare and Donne.

Buckler, William E., and Sklare, Arnold B. *Stories from Six Authors.* New York: McGraw-Hill Book Company, Inc., 1960, pp. 150-151.

Includes a "suggested interpretation" of Warren's "Blackberry Winter."

Burke, Kenneth. *The Philosophy of Literary Form: Studies in Symbolic Action.* Baton Rouge: Louisiana State University Press, 1941, pp. 79-81, 84-89; Revised edition, abridged by the author. New York: Vintage Books, 1957, pp. 67-68, 71-72, 74-75; Second edition. Baton Rouge: Louisiana State University Press, 1967, pp. 79-81, 84-89.

Includes critical comments on *Night Rider* in a discussion of the methodology of literary form.

Casper, Leonard. *Robert Penn Warren: The Dark and Bloody Ground.* Seattle: University of Washington Press, 1960.

Casper's study is a critical evaluation of Warren's works, "treated chronologically only within genres." The first book-length work on Warren, it contains the best bibliography of Warren yet in print. (Bibliography has two sections: I. "The Works of Robert Penn Warren" [Books, Textbooks and Anthologies, Short Fiction and Excerpts, Reviews and Articles, Poetry], II. "Selected Bibliography" [Criticism about Warren].)

Cottrell, Beekman W. "Cass Mastern and the Awful Responsibility of Time," *All the King's Men: A Symposium.* Pittsburgh: Carnegie Press, 1957, pp. 39-49.

Couch, W. T. (ed.) *Culture in the South.* Chapel Hill: University

of North Carolina Press, 1935, pp. 194, 197, 208.
Mentions Warren as a biographer and as a poet.

Cowan, Louise. *The Fugitive Group: A Literary History*. Baton Rouge: Louisiana State University Press, 1959.
A record and an interpretation of the "formative years" of the Fugitive poets. See index for the numerous references to Warren. [This book was developed from Cowan's Vanderbilt dissertation.]

———. "The *Pietas* of Southern Poetry," *South: Modern Southern Literature in Its Cultural Setting*. Edited by Louis D. Rubin, Jr., and Robert D. Jacobs. Garden City, New York: Doubleday & Company, Inc., 1961, pp. 95-114.
Discusses "the early Robert Penn Warren" as adhering to "the *pietas* of Southern poetry."

Cowley, Malcolm. *The Literary Situation*. New York: The Viking Press, 1958, pp. 12, 15, 160, 167.
Contains occasional references to Warren.

Daiches, David. *Critical Approaches to Literature*. Englewood Cliffs, N. J.: Prentice-Hall, Inc., 1956, pp. 160-162, 313.
Uses Warren's ideas in "Pure and Impure Poetry" to explain the function of irony in poetry; includes critical comments on *Understanding Poetry* and *Understanding Fiction*.

Davidson, Donald. *Southern Writers in the Modern World*. Athens: University of Georgia Press, 1958.
Includes three Eugenia Dorothy Blount Lamar Memorial Lectures (I. "The Thankless Muse and Her Fugitive Poets," II. "Counterattack, 1930-1940: The South Against Leviathan," III. "The Southern Writer and the Modern University"), each of which gives background material on Warren or on movements with which he is associated.

Deutsch, Babette. *Poetry in Our Time*. New York: Henry Holt and Company, 1952, pp. 188, 202-204; New York: Columbia University Press, 1956, pp. x, 188, 202-204.
Discusses Warren's themes and presents critical comments on his poetry.

———. *This Modern Poetry*. New York: W. W. Norton & Co., Inc., 1935, p. 156.

Mentions Warren, among other Fugitives, as a contributor to *I'll Take My Stand*.

*———. "Wit as the Wall," *Poetry in Our Time*. By Babette Deutsch. Second edition. Doubleday, 1963, pp. 205-241.

Douglas, Wallace W. "Deliberate Exiles: The Social Sources of Agrarian Poetics," *Aspects of American Poetry*. Edited by Richard M. Ludwig. Columbus: Ohio State University Press, 1962, pp. 273-300.

Analyzes Agrarian ideas; includes several quotations from essays by Warren.

Duncan, Joseph E. *The Revival of Metaphysical Poetry: The History of a Style, 1800 to the Present*. Minneapolis: University of Minnesota Press, 1959, pp. 186-188.

Discusses the influence of seventeenth-century metaphysical poetry on the Fugitives. Mentions several of Warren's poems as illustrations.

Eisinger, Chester E. *Fiction of the Forties*. Chicago and London: University of Chicago Press, 1963, pp. 198-229 *et passim*.

Includes the following discussions about Warren and his work:

(1) "Robert Penn Warren: The Conservative Quest for Identity";
(2) "The Background and Sources of Warren's Fiction";
(3) "Warren as His Own Critic";
(4) "The Fiction."

See index for numerous other references to Warren.

Ethridge, James M., and Kopala, Barbara (eds.). *Contemporary Authors: A Bio-Bibliographical Guide to Current Authors and Their Works*. Vols. XIII-XIV. Detroit: Gale Research Company, The Book Tower, 1965, pp. 462-463.

Includes information on these topics pertaining to Warren: Personal; Career; Awards, Honors; Writings; Sidelights; Biographical/Critical Sources.

Fain, John Tyree (ed.). *The Spyglass: Views and Reviews, 1924-1930, by Donald Davidson.* Nashville: Vanderbilt University Press, 1963, p. 259.

Indicates that Warren contributed six reviews to the book page of the *Nashville Tennessean,* Sunday edition, during the years 1924-1930.

Fiedler, Leslie A. "Three Notes on Robert Penn Warren," *No! In Thunder: Essays on Myth and Literature.* By Leslie A. Fiedler. Boston: Beacon Press, 1960, pp. 119-133.

I. "Toward Time's Cold Womb," pp. 119-126. [Originally a review of *World Enough and Time.*];

II. "Seneca in the Meat-House," pp. 127-131. [Originally a review of *Brother to Dragons.*];

III. "Fiction as Opera," pp. 131-133. [Originally a review of *Band of Angels.*].

Foster, Richard. *The New Romantics: A Reappraisal of the New Criticism.* Bloomington: Indiana University Press, 1962.

Includes quotations from and occasional comments on the following of Warren's essays: "Knowledge and the Image of Man," pp. 35, 37, 146; "A Poem of Pure Imagination," pp. 38-39; "Pure and Impure Poetry," p. 182.

Friar, Kimon, and Brinnin, John Malcolm (eds.). *Modern Poetry, American and British.* New York: Appleton-Century-Crofts, Inc., 1951, pp. 541-543.

Includes in an appendix Warren's notes on three of his poems: "Revelation," "Pursuit," and "Terror."

Garrett, George P. "The Recent Poetry of Robert Penn Warren," *Robert Penn Warren: A Collection of Critical Essays.* Edited by John Lewis Longley, Jr. New York: New York University Press, 1965, pp. 223-236.

Gerhard, George B. *Robert Penn Warren's All the King's Men.* New York: Monarch Press, Inc., 1966. (Monarch notes and study guides, No. 697-3.)

Gerstenberger, Donna, and Hendrick, George. *The American Novel, 1789-1959: A Checklist of Twentieth-Century Criticism.* Denver: Alan Swallow, 1961, pp. 252-254.

*Gettman, Royal A., and Harkness, Bruce. *Teacher's Manual for A Book of Stories*. New York: Rinehart, 1955, pp. 56-58. [On "Blackberry Winter."]

Gold, Herbert, and Stevenson, David L. (eds.) *Stories of Modern America*. New York: St. Martin's Press, 1961, pp. 96, 106.
Includes brief critical comments on "The Unvexed Isles."

Goodman, Paul. "A Southern Conceit," *Voices of Dissent*. New York: Grove Press, Inc., 1958, pp. 181-185.
A review of Warren's *Segregation: The Inner Conflict in the South*. [Reprinted from *Dissent* magazine.]

Gossett, Louise Y. *Violence in Recent Southern Fiction*. Durham, N. C.: Duke University Press, 1965, pp. 52-75 *et passim*.
Includes an essay on Warren ("Violence and the Integrity of the Self: Robert Penn Warren") and many other references to his works. (See index.)

Gregory, Horace, and Zaturenska, Marya. *A History of American Poetry 1900-1940*. New York: Harcourt, Brace and Company, 1946, pp. 383-386 *et passim*.
Includes a bio-critical sketch of Warren and his work.

*Hagopian, John V. "The Blackberry Winter," *Insight I: Analyses of American Literature*. Edited by John V. Hagopian and Martin Dolch. Frankfurt: Hirschgraben, 1962, pp. 254-259.

H[ardy], J[ohn] E[dward]. "Robert Penn Warren's 'When the Light Gets Green,'" *The Modern Talent: An Anthology of Short Stories*. By John Edward Hardy. New York: Holt Rinehart and Winston, 1964, pp. 167-173.
An analysis of and critical comments on Warren's story.

Hart, James D. *The Oxford Companion to American Literature*. First edition. New York: Oxford University Press, 1941, p. 806; Second edition, revised and enlarged. New York: Oxford University Press, 1948, p. 806; Third edition. New York: Oxford University Press, 1956, p. 806; Fourth edition. New York Oxford University Press, 1965, pp. 896-897.
All four editions contain biographical sketches of Warren. The fourth edition includes comments about his books.

Hart, John A. "Some Major Images in *All the King's Men*," *All the King's Men: A Symposium.* Pittsburgh: Carnegie Press, 1957, pp. 63-74.

Herzberg, Max J. *The Reader's Encyclopedia of American Literature.* New York: Thomas Y. Crowell Company, 1962, p. 1197.
A bio-critical sketch.

Hoffman, Frederick J. *The Modern Novel in America 1900-1950.* Chicago: Henry Regnery Company, 1951, pp. 197-200 *et passim*; *Chicago: Henry Regnery, 1956.
Includes critical discussions of *Night Rider*, *At Heaven's Gate*, *All the King's Men*, and *World Enough and Time;* contains a few other passing references to Warren's works.

———, Allen, Charles, and Ulrich, Carolyn F. *The Little Magazine.* Princeton: Princeton University Press, 1946.
Includes critical and biographical comments on Warren; also mentions Warren in connection with many "little magazines" with which he was associated.

Holman, C. Hugh. "The Defense of Art: Criticism Since 1930," *The Development of American Literary Criticism.* Edited by Floyd Stovall. Chapel Hill: University of North Carolina Press, 1955, pp. 231, 237.
Mentions Warren's impact on literary criticism.

Howard, Leon. *Literature and the American Tradition.* Garden City, New York: Doubleday & Company, Inc., 1960, p. 313.
Includes a brief discussion of *All the King's Men.*

Humphrey, Robert. *Stream of Consciousness in the Modern Novel.* Berkeley: University of California Press, 1954, pp. 114-117.
Discusses *All the King's Men* and *World Enough and Time* as examples of the "pervading influence of the stream-of-consciousness genre on recent fiction."

Hyman, Stanley Edgar. *The Armed Vision: A Study in the Methods of Modern Literary Criticism.* New York: Alfred A. Knopf, 1948.

See index for the many scattered references to Warren's contributions to literary criticism.

Jones, Howard Mumford. *Guide to American Literature and Its Backgrounds Since 1890.* Cambridge: Harvard University Press, 1953, pp. 32, 40, 44; Second edition, revised. Cambridge: Harvard University Press, 1959; Third edition. By Howard Mumford Jones and Richard M. Ludwig. Cambridge: Harvard University Press, 1964, pp. 77, 177, 184, 210.

Joost, Nicholas. " 'Was All For Naught?': Robert Penn Warren and New Directions in the Novel," *Fifty Years of the American Novel: A Christian Appraisal.* Edited by Harold C. Gardiner, S. J. New York: Charles Scribner's Sons, 1951, pp. 273-291.

Kallsen, Loren J. (ed.) *The Kentucky Tragedy: A Problem in Romantic Attitudes.* Indianapolis and New York: Bobbs-Merrill Company, Inc., 1963.

Contains the four primary documents pertaining to the murder of Colonel Solomon Sharp by Jereboam O. Beauchamp. (Warren's *World Enough and Time* is based on this murder, known as the "Kentucky tragedy.")

Karanikas, Alexander. *Tillers of a Myth: Southern Agrarians as Social and Literary Critics.* Madison: University of Wisconsin Press, 1966.

See index for many references to Warren in Karanikas's outline and evaluation of the development of the Southern Agrarians (who were first Fugitive poets, later Southern Agrarians, and finally New Critics).

Kreymborg, Alfred. *Our Singing Strength: An Outline of American Poetry (1620-1930).* New York: Coward-McCann, Inc., 1929, pp. 565-567.

Includes critical comments on Warren's poetry.

Kunitz, Stanley J., and Haycraft, Howard (eds.). *Twentieth Century Authors.* New York: The H. W. Wilson Company, 1942, pp. 1476-1477; First supplement. Edited by Stanley J. Kunitz and Vineta Colby. New York: The H. W. Wilson Company, 1955, pp. 1050-1051.

First edition includes a biographical and an autobiographical sketch of Warren. (Autobiographical sketch is almost identical to that one appearing in the *Wilson Bulletin,* XIII (May, 1939), 652.) First supplement contains a bio-critical sketch of Warren.

Leary, Lewis (ed.). *Contemporary Literary Scholarship: A Critical Review.* New York: Appleton-Century-Crofts, Inc., 1958, pp. 218, 227, 253-254.

Includes scattered references to Warren's contributions to literary scholarship.

Levin, Harry. *Contexts of Criticism.* Cambridge: Harvard University Press, 1957, pp. 142, 149, 153.

Includes comments on Warren's criticism of Hemingway.

Longley, John Lewis, Jr. (ed.) *Robert Penn Warren: A Collection of Critical Essays.* New York: New York University Press, 1965. Includes the following:

1. "Robert Penn Warren's Novels: The Symbolic and Textural Patterns," by John M. Bradbury;
2. "The Art of Fiction XVIII: Robert Penn Warren," by Ralph Ellison and Eugene Walter;
3. "Robert Penn Warren's *Night Rider*: The Nihilism of the Isolated Temperament," by Alvan S. Ryan;
4. "Self-Knowledge, the Pearl of Pus, and the Seventh Circle: The Major Themes in *At Heaven's Gate,*" by John Lewis Longley, Jr.;
5. "All the King's Men: The Matrix of Experience," by Robert Penn Warren;
6. "Melpomene as Wallflower; or, The Reading of Tragedy," by Robert B. Heilman;
7. "Tangled Web," by Robert B. Heilman;
8. "The Romantic Tragedy of Self in *World Enough and Time,*" by Frederick P. W. McDowell;
9. "Mr. Warren and the Reviewers," by F. Cudworth Flint;
10. "Miscegenation as Symbol: *Band of Angels,*" by Leonard Casper;
11. "Journey to the Interior," by Leonard Casper;
12. "Trial by Wilderness: Warren's Exemplum," by Leonard Casper;

13. "When All is Said and Done: Warren's *Flood*," by John Lewis Longley, Jr.;
14. "The Burden of the Literary Mind: Some Meditations on Robert Penn Warren as Historian," by William C. Havard;
15. "Psychology and Theme in *Brother to Dragons*," by Frederick P. W. McDowell;
16. "The Recent Poetry of Robert Penn Warren," by George P. Garrett;
17. "Knowledge and the Image of Man," by Robert Penn Warren.

Those essays numbered 13 and 16 were first published in this volume.

———. "When All Is Said and Done: Warren's *Flood*," *Robert Penn Warren: A Collection of Critical Essays*. Edited by John Lewis Longley, Jr. New York: New York University Press, 1965, pp. 169-177.

Ludwig, Richard M. (ed.) *Literary History of the United States: Bibliography Supplement*. New York: The Macmillan Company, 1959, pp. 234-236; Third edition, revised. Edited by Robert E. Spiller *et al.* New York: The Macmillan Company, 1963, pp. 234-236 of *Bibliography Supplement*.

Both editions include a Warren bibliography covering separate works by him, and a biography and criticism of him.

Magill, Frank N. (ed.) *Cyclopedia of World Authors*. New York: Harper & Brothers, 1958, pp. 1126-1128.

A bio-critical sketch of Warren. Includes a selected bibliography of criticism about him.

Matthiessen, F. O. "Four American Poets, 1944," *The Responsibilities of the Critic: Essays and Reviews*. By F. O. Matthiessen. New York: Oxford University Press, 1952, pp. 121-124.

Includes a review of Warren's *Selected Poems: 1923-1943*.

Millett, Fred B. *Contemporary American Authors: A Critical Survey and 219 Bio-Bibliographies*. New York: Harcourt, Brace and Company, 1940, pp. 147, 628-629.

Mims, Edwin. *The Advancing South.* Garden City: Doubleday, Page & Company, 1926, pp. 198-201.
Mentions Warren in a discussion of the Fugitive movement.

———. *History of Vanderbilt University.* Nashville: Vanderbilt University Press, 1946, pp. 415, 416 (footnote).
Mentions Warren as a Fugitive Poet and as an occupant of the Chair of Poetry at the Library of Congress.

Mohrt, Michel. *Le nouveau roman américain.* Paris: Gallimard, 1955, pp. 201-206, 207-223.
Includes critical comments on Warren (pp. 201-206), and an essay about him ("Robert Penn Warren ou Le Mythe Du Hors-La-Loi," pp. 207-223). In French.

Monroe, Harriet. *A Poet's Life.* New York: The Macmillan Company, 1938, p. 430.
Designates Warren, Ransom, Tate, and Davidson as "southern regionalists."

Moore, Merrill. *The Fugitive: Clippings and Comment.* Collected by Merrill Moore. Boston: Privately printed, 1939.
Moore's book is "not the story of *The Fugitive.* It is merely a disjointed, but chronologically (approximately) regular report of some (not all) of the clippings and comment about *The Fugitive* that appeared in newspapers and periodicals, mostly local."
Includes *many* scattered references to Warren.

The National Cyclopaedia of American Biography. Current Volume H, 1947-52. New York: James T. White & Company, 1952, p. 332.
Biographical sketch of Warren.

Nyren, Dorothy (ed.). *A Library of Literary Criticism: Modern American Literature.* New York: Frederick Ungar Publishing Co., 1960, pp. 503-508; Second edition. New York: Frederick Ungar Publishing Co., 1961, pp. 503-508, 576; Third edition. New York: Frederick Ungar Publishing Co., 1964, pp. 503-508, 587-589.
All editions contain excerpts from important critical appraisals

of Warren. Second and third editions have an index indicating excerpts from Warren's critical writings included in the volumes.

O'Connor, William Van. *An Age of Criticism: 1900-1950.* Chicago: Henry Regnery Company, 1952, pp. 108, 157, 165-166, 170-171, 175.

Includes quotations from and comments about Warren's criticism; concludes with a "fable" about critics by Warren.

———. "Robert Penn Warren, 'Provincial' Poet," *A Southern Vanguard.* Edited by Allen Tate. New York: Prentice-Hall, Inc., 1947, pp. 92-99.

———. *Sense and Sensibility in Modern Poetry.* Chicago: University of Chicago Press, 1948, pp. 89-90, 145-146, 154-155, *et passim.*

Includes discussions of Warren's theories of poetry, analyses of some of his poems, and quotations from his essays.

Parks, Edd Winfield. *Segments of Southern Thought.* Athens: University of Georgia Press, 1938, pp. 72, 106, 115-119.

Contains passing references to Warren, quotations from his essays, and a critical estimate of him: ". . . he seems a poet of magnificent promise rather than of positive achievement, except in the sequence, 'Kentucky Mountain Farm.' "

———. *Southern Poets: Representative Selections.* New York: American Book Company, 1936, pp. cxxiv-cxxviii.

Mentions Warren's membership in the Fugitive group and characterizes him as "a poet of magnificent promise rather than of positive achievement."

*Poenicke, Klaus. *Robert Penn Warren: Kuntswerk und Kritische Theorie.* (Beihefte zum Jahrbuch für Amerikastudien, No. 4.) Heidelberg: Carl Winter, 1959.

Pratt, William. "In Pursuit of the Fugitives," *The Fugitive Poets: Modern Southern Poetry in Perspective.* Edited by William Pratt. New York: E. P. Dutton & Co., Inc., 1965, pp. 13-46.

Includes a critical assessment of Warren, in addition to a general history of the Fugitive movement.

Prescott, Orville. "The Political Novel: Warren, Orwell, Koestler," *In My Opinion*. By Orville Prescott. Indianapolis and New York: Bobbs-Merrill Company, Inc., 1952, pp. 24-27.

Examines *All the King's Men* and *World Enough and Time* as exemplary of one of the two main types of political fiction.

Pritchard, John Paul. *Criticism in America: An Account of the Development of Critical Techniques from the Early Period of the Republic to the Middle Years of the Twentieth Century*. Norman, Oklahoma: University of Oklahoma Press, 1956, p. 251.

Comments on *Understanding Poetry* (1938).

Purdy, Rob Roy (ed.). *Fugitives' Reunion: Conversations at Vanderbilt*. Nashville: Vanderbilt University Press, 1959.

A transcript of the recorded conversations of the Fugitives during their reunion at Vanderbilt, May 3-5, 1956. Includes an introduction by Louis D. Rubin, Jr.

Quinn, Arthur Hobson (ed.). *The Literature of the American People*. New York: Appleton-Century-Crofts, Inc., 1951, pp. 922, 924.

Mentions Warren in his discussion of the Fugitives.

Raiziss, Sona. *The Metaphysical Passion: Seven Modern American Poets and the Seventeenth-Century Tradition*. Philadelphia: University of Pennsylvania Press, 1952, pp. 196-203 *et passim*.

Includes a detailed analysis of the metaphysical elements in Warren's poetry.

Rock, Virginia. "The Twelve Southerners: Biographical Essays," *I'll Take My Stand: The South and the Agrarian Tradition*. By Twelve Southerners. New York: Harper Torchbooks, 1962, pp. 360-363, 381-383.

Contains general comments on the Agrarians as a group, as well as biographical and critical observations about Warren.

Rosenthal, M. L. *The Modern Poets: A Critical Introduction*. New York: Oxford University Press, 1960, pp. 250-252; New York: Oxford University Press, 1965, pp. 250-252.

Both editions discuss Warren as "one of a group of poets

who, with lively vigor, combine modern technique and sensibility with a more public appeal than is usual among their peers."

Rossiter, Clinton. *Conservatism in America.* New York: Alfred A. Knopf, 1955, pp. 206-207; New York: Vintage Books, 1962, pp. 228-232.

Mentions Warren in connection with *I'll Take My Stand.*

Rubin, Louis D., Jr. *The Faraway Country: Writers of the Modern South.* Seattle: University of Washington Press, 1963, pp. 11-13, 15, 98, 105-130, 155-161, 176-184, 235, *et passim.*

Rubin studies the influence of the South on Warren's work; he devotes to Warren an entire chapter ("Burden's Landing: *All the King's Men* and the Modern South"), as well as *many* other pages of discussion.

———, and Jacobs, Robert D. (eds.) *South: Modern Southern Literature in its Cultural Setting.* Garden City, New York: Doubleday & Company, Inc., 1961, pp. 198-209, 425-428. (Dolphin Books.)

Includes an essay about Warren ("Robert Penn Warren," by Ellington White), and a Warren bibliography in four sections (1. Books by Warren, 2. Children's Books by Warren, 3. Textbooks and Books Edited by Warren, 4. About Warren).

———, and ——— (eds.) *Southern Renascence:* The Literature of the Modern South. Baltimore: The Johns Hopkins Press, 1953, pp. 207-224, 225-235, *et passim.*

Includes two essays on Warren (1. "Violence and Order in the Novels of Robert Penn Warren," by Charles R. Anderson; 2. "Warren as Philosopher in *World Enough and Time,*" by Harry Modean Campbell), as well as many other *significant* references to Warren. (See index.)

*Sale, William M., Jr., Hall, James, and Steinman, Martin, Jr. *Critical Discussions for Teachers Using "Short Stories: Tradition and Direction."* Norfolk: New Directions, 1949, pp. 48-50.

On "The Patented Gate and the Mean Hamburger."

Schramm, Wilbur L. *Literary Scholarship: Its Aims and Methods.*

Chapel Hill: University of North Carolina Press, 1941, pp. 199, 203, 205.

Mentions Warren's studying at Oxford, his founding a small quarterly, and his belonging to the Fugitive group at Vanderbilt.

Schutte, William M. "The Dramatic Versions of the Willie Stark Story," *All the King's Men: A Symposium*. Pittsburgh: Carnegie Press, 1957, pp. 75-90.

Scott, Wilbur S. *Five Approaches of Literary Criticism: An Arrangement of Contemporary Critical Essays*. New York: The Macmillan Company, 1962, pp. 110, 113-114, 181, 184.

Mentions Warren's "Pure and Impure Poetry," and Brooks and Warren's analysis of Sherwood Anderson's "I Want to Know Why."

Slack, Robert C. "The Telemachus Theme," *All the King's Men: A Symposium*. Pittsburgh: Carnegie Press, 1957, pp. 29-38.

Sochatoff, A. Fred. "Some Treatments of the Huey Long Theme," *All the King's Men: A Symposium*. Pittsburgh: Carnegie Press, 1957, pp. 3-15.

Southworth, James G. *More Modern American Poets*. Oxford: Basil Blackwell, 1954, pp. 114-119.

Includes a chapter entitled "Robert Penn Warren," in which Southworth analyzes several of Warren's poems and offers a critical estimate of Warren's poetry in general.

Spiller, Robert E., *et al. Literary History of the United States*. New York: The Macmillan Company, 1948, p. 1347; Revised edition. New York: The Macmillan Company, 1953, p. 1347; Third edition, revised. New York: The Macmillan Company, 1963, pp. 1347, 1404-1405.

All editions include critical comments on Warren's poetry, and other passing references to Warren; third edition adds criticism of his novels.

Stallman, Robert Wooster (ed.). *The Critic's Notebook*. Minneapolis: University of Minnesota Press, 1950, pp. 105-106, 112-113, 163, 210-211, 213, 226-228.

Includes several quotations from Warren's "A Poem of Pure Imagination: An Experiment in Reading."

———. "The New Criticism and the Southern Critics," *A Southern Vanguard*. Edited by Allen Tate. New York: Prentice-Hall, Inc., 1947, pp. 28-51.

Mentions Warren as one of the Southern critics whose "achievement in criticism . . . has not been equaled by literary critics in our time or in any previous period of our literary history."

Steinberg, Erwin R. "The Enigma of Willie Stark," *All the King's Men: A Symposium*. Pittsburgh: Carnegie Press, 1957, pp. 17-28.

Stewart, John L. *The Burden of Time: The Fugitives and Agrarians*. Princeton, New Jersey: Princeton University Press, 1965, pp. 3-205, 427-542.

Includes chapters on the Fugitives and on Agrarianism, in addition to two chapters devoted exclusively to Warren: (1) "Robert Penn Warren: The Long Apprenticeship," and (2) "Robert Penn Warren: The Achievement." See detailed index for explicit references to Warren's fiction, poetry, and other writing; and for general references to Warren.

Stewart, Randall. *American Literature and Christian Doctrine*. Baton Rouge: Louisiana State University Press, 1958, pp. 40-42, 142-146, *et passim*.

Includes comments on *Brother to Dragons*, *All the King's Men*, *Night Rider*, and "Original Sin: A Short Story," in addition to other statements about Warren's philosophy.

Strandberg, Victor H. *A Colder Fire: The Poetry of Robert Penn Warren*. Lexington: University of Kentucky Press, 1965.
Includes the following chapters:
Introduction
The Themes of Robert Penn Warren
Chapter One
The Emerging of Vision and Voice:
Selected Poems: 1923-1943 and Its Sources

Thirty-six Poems: The Dark Night of Naturalism
Eleven Poems on the Same Theme:
The Undiscovered Self
Three "New" Poems: The Dead End of Naturalism
Chapter Two
Brother to Dragons: "Warren's Best Book"
Chapter Three
Promises: A Legacy
The Rosanna Poems
The Promise to Gabriel: Oneness of Time and Flesh
Chapter Four
You, Emperors, and Others: A Culmination

Straumann, Heinrich. *American Literature in the Twentieth Century*. London: Hutchinson's University Library, 1951, pp. 114-117 *et passim;* Third revised edition. New York: Harper & Row, 1965, pp. 120-123 *et passim* (Harper Torchbooks).
Contains general critical comments on Warren's work, in addition to specific comments about *Night Rider*, *At Heaven's Gate*, and *All the King's Men.*

Sutton, Walter. *Modern Amercian Criticism.* Englewood Cliffs: Prentice-Hall, Inc., 1963.
Includes passing references to Warren's contributions to American literary criticism.

Tate, Allen. *On the Limits of Poetry: Selected Essays: 1928-1948.* New York: The Swallow Press and William Morrow & Company, 1948, pp. 176, 180, 200, 292.
Includes scattered comments by and about Warren.

———. *Recent American Poetry and Poetic Criticism.* Washington: Library of Congress, 1943, p. 9.
Lists Warren's *Eleven Poems on the Same Theme* and makes a critical comment about his work.

———. *Sixty American Poets, 1896-1944.* Washington: Library of Congress, 1945, pp. 173-174; Revised edition. Washington: Library of Congress, 1954, pp. 140-142.
Includes a brief critical statement about Warren, and a bibliography of works by him.

Thorp, Willard. *American Writing in the Twentieth Century*. Cambridge: Harvard University Press, 1960, pp. 252-254 *et passim.*

Includes a discussion of Warren's philosophy as expressed in his writing; contains several references to Warren's contributions to twentieth-century writing.

Thurston, Jarvis, *et al. Short Fiction Criticism: A Checklist of Interpretation since 1925 of Stories and Novelettes*. Denver: Alan Swallow, 1960, p. 196.

Untermeyer, Louis (ed.) *Modern American Poetry: A Critical Anthology*. Fourth revised edition. New York: Harcourt, Brace and Company, 1930, pp. 30, 811; Fifth revised edition. New York: Harcourt, Brace and Company, 1936, pp. 621-622 *et passim;* Sixth revised edition. New York: Harcourt, Brace and Company, 1942, pp. 668-669. Reprinted as *Modern American Poetry*. Mid-Century edition. New York: Harcourt, Brace and Company, 1950, pp. 25, 618-619; New and enlarged edition. New York: Harcourt, Brace & World, Inc., 1962, pp. 581-582.

All editions include brief critical comment on Warren's work.

——— (ed.) *Modern American Poetry, Modern British Poetry: A Critical Anthology*. Combined edition. New York: Harcourt, Brace and Company, 1942, pp. 668-676. Reprinted as *Modern American Poetry, Modern British Poetry*. Combined mid-century edition. New York: Harcourt, Brace and Company, 1950, pp. 25, 618-619; Combined new and enlarged edition. New York: Harcourt, Brace & World, Inc., 1962, pp. 581-582.

All editions include brief critical comment on Warren's work.

Vivas, Eliseo. *The Artistic Transaction and Essays on Theory of Literature*. Columbus: Ohio State University Press, 1963, pp. 172, 244.

Includes a passing reference to Warren as a "contextualist critic"; mentions Elder Olson's review of Warren's "A Poem of Pure Imagination: An Experiment in Reading."

Wagenknecht, Edward. *Cavalcade of the American Novel.* New York: Henry Holt and Company, 1952, pp. 456-457, 555.

Contains a critical estimate of Warren's novels and a brief bibliography of critical discussions of his novels.

Walcutt, Charles Child, and Whitesell, J. Edwin (eds.). *The Explicator Cyclopedia.* Chicago: Quadrangle Books, 1966, Vol. I, pp. 336-339.

Reprints the following three articles from *The Explicator,* Vols. I-XX (1942-1962):

1. "Original Sin: A Short Story," by Richard E. Amacher, VIII (May, 1950), Item 52;
2. "Original Sin: A Short Story," by Clifford M. Gordon, IX (December, 1950), Item 21;
3. "Pursuit," by William Frost, XI (February, 1953), Item 22.

Walker, Warren S. (compiler) *Twentieth-Century Short Story Explication: Interpretations, 1900-1960 Inclusive, of Short Fiction Since 1800.* Hamden, Connecticut: The Shoe String Press, Inc., 1961, pp. 347-348.

See *Supplement I* for interpretations between 1960 and April 1, 1963; *Supplement II* for interpretations from April 1, 1963 through December 31, 1964.

Walker, William E., and Welker, Robert L. (ed.). *Reality and Myth: Essays in American Literature in Memory of Richmond Croom Beatty.* Nashville: Vanderbilt University Press, 1964, pp. 193, 194 (footnote), 196, 197, 199, 213, 272.

Includes several allusions to Warren's ideas and works; quotes from two essays by Warren.

Warfel, Harry R. *American Novelists of Today.* New York: American Book Company, 1951, pp. 442-443.

Biographical sketch of Warren.

Wasserstrom, William. *Heiress of All the Ages: Sex and Sentiment in the Genteel Tradition.* Minneapolis: University of Minnesota Press, 1959, pp. 114-122 *et passim.*

In this study of the role of women in fiction, Wasserstrom

incorporates discussions of *Night Rider, At Heaven's Gate, All the King's Men, World Enough and Time,* and *Band of Angels.*

Wellek, René. *Concepts of Criticism.* Edited by Stephen G. Nichols, Jr. New Haven: Yale University Press, 1963.
See index for passing references to Warren.

———, and Warren, Austin. *Theory of Literature.* New York: Harcourt, Brace and Company, 1949, p. 260.
Mentions Brooks and Warren's belief that one should first judge, then " 'place' " a poem "as to author, period, or school. . . ."

Wells, Henry W. *New Poets from Old.* New York: Columbia University Press, 1940, pp. 9, 187.
Mentions Warren's interest in his poetic forerunners; also notes that Warren has several times used the verse epistle "with distinction."

West, Paul. *Robert Penn Warren.* Minneapolis: University of Minnesota Press, 1964; London: Oxford University Press, 1965. (University of Minnesota Pamphlets on American Writers, No. 44.)
A bio-critical sketch of Warren. Contains a selected bibliography of works by and about him.

West, Ray B., Jr. *The Short Story in America 1900-1950.* Chicago: Henry Regnery Company, 1952, pp. 77-80 *et passim.*
Contains a critical analysis of "Blackberry Winter," and several brief references to Warren and his other work.

White, Ellington. "Robert Penn Warren," *South: Modern Southern Literature in Its Cultural Setting.* Edited by Louis D. Rubin, Jr., and Robert D. Jacobs. Garden City, New York: Doubleday & Company, Inc., 1961, pp. 198-209. (Dolphin Books.)
Discusses Warren's "concern with man as a political animal."

Wilder, Amos N. *Theology and Modern Literature.* Cambridge: Harvard University Press, 1958, pp. 23, 27, 33.
Includes critical comments on *Brother to Dragons* and a quotation by Warren.

Williamson, George. "Donne and the Poetry of Today," *A Garland for John Donne, 1631-1931*. Edited by Theodore Spencer. Cambridge: Harvard University Press, 1931, pp. 155-176.

Mentions the influence of Donne on the Fugitives; however, does not cite Warren specifically.

Wimsatt, William K., Jr., and Brooks, Cleanth. *Literary Criticism: A Short History*. New York: Alfred A. Knopf, 1957, pp. 646-648, 651, 675.

Includes ideas and quotations from Warren's "Pure and Impure Poetry."

Woodruff, Neal, Jr. "The Technique of *All the King's Men*," *All the King's Men: A Symposium*. Pittsburgh: Carnegie Press, 1957, pp. 51-62.

Young, Thomas Daniel, Watkins, Floyd C., and Beatty, Richmond Croom. *The Literature of the South*. Revised edition. Glenview, Illinois: Scott, Foresman and Company, 1968, pp. 614-617, 1042-1043, *et passim*.

Includes discussions of Warren's contributions to Southern literature, as well as critical evaluation of his work. (See index for scattered references to Warren.)

PERIODICALS

"*All the King's Men:* A Symposium," *Folio*, XV (May, 1950), 2-22.

Allen, Charles. "The Fugitive," *South Atlantic Quarterly*, XLIII (October, 1944), 382-389.

Allen, Charles A. "Robert Penn Warren: The Psychology of Self-Knowlelge," *Literature and Psychology*, VIII (Spring, 1958), 21-25.

Amacher, Richard E. "Warren's *Original Sin: A Short Story*," *Explicator*, VIII (May, 1950), Item 52. Reprinted in *The Explicator Cyclopedia*. Edited by Charles Child Walcutt and J. Edwin Whitesell. Chicago: Quadrangle Books, 1966, Vol. I, pp. 336-337.

Anderson, Charles R. "Violence and Order in the Novels of Robert Penn Warren," *Hopkins Review*, VI (Winter, 1953), 88-105. Reprinted in the following:

Southern Renascence: The Literature of the Modern South. Edited by Louis D. Rubin, Jr., and Robert D. Jacobs. Baltimore: Johns Hopkins Press, 1953, pp. 207-224;

Modern American Fiction: Essays in Criticism. Edited by A. Walton Litz. New York: Oxford University Press, 1963, pp. 278-295.

Annual Report of the Librarian of Congress for the Fiscal Year Ended June 30, 1944. Washington: United States Government Printing Office, 1945, pp. 36, 60.

Notes that Warren succeeded Allen Tate as Consultant in Poetry in English at the Library of Congress (an office which Warren held during fiscal year 1945), and as editor of *The Library of Congress Quarterly Journal of Current Acquisitions.*

Annual Report of the Librarian of Congress for the Fiscal Year Ended June 30, 1945. Washington: United States Government Printing Office, 1946, pp. 30, 90, 147-148.

Surveys Warren's accomplishments as Consultant in Poetry in English at the Library of Congress.

*Antonini, Giacomo. "Il mito della dignità umana. Penn Warren: Nostalgia per il vecchio Sud," *La Fiera Letteraria*, No. 4 (January 22, 1956), 1-2.

*———. "Il Sud di Robert Penn Warren," *La Fiera Letteraria*, XVII (October 21, 1962), 1, 3.

*———. Penn Warrent e il primato dello stile," *La Fiera Letteraria*, No. 1 (January 12, 1955), 5-6.

Baker, Carlos. "Souls Lost in a Blind Lobby," *Saturday Review*, XXXVIII (August 20, 1955), 9-10.

Baker, Joseph E. "Irony in Fiction: *All the King's Men*," *College English*, IX (December, 1947), 112-130.

Barker, George. "Red Warren, Rebel in the Ivy League," *Nashville Tennessean Magazine*, December 27, 1964, pp. 6-7.

*Barucca, Primo. "La caverna di Warren," *La Fiera Letteraria*, XVI (June 18, 1961), 4.

Basso, Hamilton. "The Huey Long Legend," *Life*, XXI (December 9, 1946), 106-108, 110, 112, 115-116, 118, 121.

Beardsley, Monroe C. "The New Criticism Revisited: An Affirmative View," *Four Quarters*, XIII (January, 1964), 11-19.

Beatty, Richmond Croom. "Fugitive and Agrarian Writers at Vanderbilt," *Tennessee Historical Quarterly*, III (March, 1944), 3-23. Reprinted in revised form as "By Way of Background" in *A Vanderbilt Miscellany 1919-1944*. Edited by Richmond Croom Beatty. Nashville: Vanderbilt University Press, 1944, pp. 11-27.

______. "A Personal Memoir of the Agrarians," *Shenandoah*, III (Summer, 1952), 11-13.

Beebe, Keith. "Biblical Motifs in *All the King's Men*," *Journal of Bible and Religion*, XXX (April, 1962), 123-130.

Beebe, Maurice, and Marcus, Erin. "Criticism of Robert Penn Warren: A Selected Checklist," *Modern Fiction Studies*, VI (Spring, 1960), 83-88.

Bentley, Eric. "All the King's Men," *Theatre Arts*, XXXI (November, 1947), 72-73.

______. "The Meaning of Robert Penn Warren's Novels," *Kenyon Review*, X (Summer, 1948), 407-424. Reprinted in the following:
Forms of Modern Fiction: Essays Collected in Honor of Joseph Warren Beach. Edited by William Van O'Connor. Minneapolis: University of Minnesota Press, 1948, pp. 269-286;

**On Contemporary Literature*. Edited by Richard Kostelanetz. Avon Books, 1964, pp. 616-633.

Berner, Robert. "The Required Past: *World Enough and Time*," *Modern Fiction Studies*, VI (Spring, 1960), 55-64.

Blonski, Jan. "Robert Penn Warren," *Tworczosc*, XII (Marzec, 1956), 164-167. (In Polish.)

Blum, Morgan. "Promises as Fulfillment," *Kenyon Review,* XXI (Winter, 1959), 97-120.

Bradbury, John M. "Robert Penn Warren's Novels: The Symbolic and Textural Patterns," *Accent,* XIII (Spring, 1953), 77-89. Reprinted in *Robert Penn Warren: A Collection of Critical Essays.* Edited by John Lewis Longley, Jr. New York: New York University Press, 1965, pp. 3-17. Reprinted in revised and enlarged form as "Warren's Fiction" in *The Fugitives: A Critical Account.* By John M. Bradbury. Chapel Hill: University of North Carolina Press, 1958, pp. 195-230.

———. "Warren's Fiction." See "Robert Penn Warren's Novels: The Symbolic and Textural Patterns."

Breit, Harvey. "Robert Penn Warren." See "Talk with Mr. Warren."

———. "Talk with Mr. Warren," *New York Times Book Review,* June 25, 1950, p. 20. Reprinted as "Robert Penn Warren" in *The Writer Observed.* By Harvey Breit. Cleveland and New York: World Publishing Company, 1956, pp. 131-133.

Brooks, Cleanth. "The Modern Southern Poet and Tradition," *Virginia Quarterly Review,* XI (April, 1935), 305-320.

———. "Regionalism in American Literature," *Journal of Southern History,* XXVI (February, 1960), 35-43.

Byrne, Clifford M. "The Philosophical Development in Four of Robert Penn Warren's Novels," *McNeese Review,* IX (Winter, 1957), 56-68.

Campbell, Harry Modean. "Notes on Religion in the Southern Renascence," *Shenandoah,* VI (Summer, 1955), 10-18.

———. "Warren as Philosopher in *World Enough and Time,*" *Hopkins Review,* VI (Winter, 1953), 106-116. Reprinted in *Southern Renascence: The Literature of the Modern South.* Edited by Louis D. Rubin, Jr., and Robert D. Jacobs. Baltimore: Johns Hopkins Press, 1953, pp. 225-235.

Cargill, Oscar. "Anatomist of Monsters," *College English,* IX

(October, 1947), 1-8. Reprinted with an "Afterword" in *Toward a Pluralistic Criticism.* By Oscar Cargill. Carbondale: Southern Illinois University Press, 1965, pp. 141-153.

Carter, Everett. "The 'Little Myth' of Robert Penn Warren," *Modern Fiction Studies,* VI (Spring, 1960), 3-12.

Casper, Leonard. "The Fallacy of Heresy," *Western Review,* XXIII (Spring, 1959), 283-287.

———. "The Founding Fathers," *Western Review,* XXII (Autumn, 1957), 69-71. Reprinted in modified form in *Robert Penn Warren: The Dark and Bloody Ground.* By Leonard Casper. Seattle: University of Washington Press, 1960.

———. "Golden Eye, Unwinking," *Perspective,* X (Winter, 1959), 201-208. Reprinted in modified form in *Robert Penn Warren: The Dark and Bloody Ground.* By Leonard Casper. Seattle: University of Washington Press, 1960.

———. "Journey to the Interior: *The Cave,*" *Modern Fiction Studies,* VI (Spring, 1960), 65-72. Reprinted in *Robert Penn Warren: A Collection of Critical Essays.* Edited by John Lewis Longley, Jr. New York: New York University Press, 1965, pp. 149-158.

*———. "Mirror for Mobs: The Willie Stark Stories," *Drama Critique,* II (November, 1959), 120-124. Reprinted in modified form in *Robert Penn Warren: The Dark and Bloody Ground.* By Leonard Casper, Seattle: University of Washington Press, 1960.

———. "Miscegenation as Symbol: *Band of Angels,*" *Audience,* VI (Autumn, 1959), 66-74. Reprinted in modified form in *Robert Penn Warren: The Dark and Bloody Ground.* By Leonard Casper. Seattle: University of Washington Press, 1960. Reprinted in *Robert Penn Warren: A Collection of Critical Essays.* Edited by John Lewis Longley, Jr. New York: New York University Press, 1965, pp. 140-148.

———. "The New Criticism and Southern Agrarianism," *Diliman Review* [Philippines], II (April, 1954), 136-149.

———. "Robert Penn Warren: An Assessment," *Diliman Review* [Philippines], II (October, 1954), 400-424.

———. "Robert Penn Warren: Method and Canon," *Diliman Review* [Philippines], II (July, 1954), 263-292.

———. "Trial by Wilderness: Warren's Exemplum," *Wisconsin Studies in Contemporary Literature*, III (Fall, 1962), 45-53. Reprinted in *Robert Penn Warren: A Collection of Critical Essays*. Edited by John Lewis Longley, Jr. New York: New York University Press, 1965, pp. 159-168.

———. "Warren and the Unsuspecting Ancestor," *Wisconsin Studies in Contemporary Literature*, II (Spring-Summer, 1961), 43-49.

Cater, Catherine. "Four Voices Out of the South," *Michigan Alumnus Quarterly Review*, L (Winter, 1944), pp. 166-173.

Cheney, Brainard. "Is There a Voice Unheard in Warren's Book Who is Speaking for the Negro?" *Sewanee Review*, LXXIV (Spring, 1966), 545-550.

Chrismer, Wayde. "The Civil War Centennial—An Appraisal of Its Literature," *American Book Collector*, XVI (May, 1966), 9-11.

*Clark, Marden J. "Religious Implications in the Novels of Robert Penn Warren," *Brigham Young University Studies*, IV (Autumn, 1961), 67-79.

Clements, A. L. "Theme and Reality in *At Heaven's Gate* and *All the King's Men*," *Criticism*, V (Winter, 1963), 27-44.

Connelly, Thomas Lawrence. "The Vanderbilt Agrarians: Time and Place in Southern Tradition," *Tennessee Historical Quarterly*, XXII (March, 1963), 22-37.

Cowan, Louise. "The Communal World of Southern Literature," *Georgia Review*, XIV (Fall, 1960), 248-257.

Crane, R. S. "Cleanth Brooks; or, the Bankruptcy of Critical Monism," *Modern Philology*, XLV (May, 1948), 226-245.
Mentions Warren's "obsession with symbols" in a discussion

of the ". . . tendency toward a monistic reduction of critical concepts. . . ."

Crisler, B. R. "Again the Troublous Saga of Willie Stark," *Christian Science Monitor Magazine Section,* July 22, 1950, p. 7.
Review of a staging of *All the King's Men* at the President Theater in New York.

Current-Garcia, Eugene. "The Fugitive Agrarian Movement: A Symposium Introduction," *Mississippi Quarterly,* XIII (Spring, 1960), 53-54.

Daniel, Robert. "The Critics of Nashville," *Tennessee Studies in Literature,* I (1956), 19-26.

———. "No Place to Go," *Sewanee Review,* LVI (Summer, 1948), 524-526.
On *The Circus in the Attic.*

Davidson, Donald. " 'I'll Take My Stand': A History," *American Review,* V (Summer, 1935), 301-321.

———. "The Thankless Muse and Her Fugitive Poets," *Sewanee Review,* LXVI (Spring, 1958), 201-228. Reprinted in *Southern Writers in the Modern World.* By Donald Davidson. Athens: University of Georgia Press, 1958, pp. 1-30.

Davis, Joe. "Robert Penn Warren and the Journey to the West," *Modern Fiction Studies,* VI (Spring, 1960), 73-82.

Douglas, Wallace W. "Drug Store Gothic: The Style of Robert Penn Warren," *College English,* XV (February, 1954), 265-272.

Dwyer, William F. "Light Religiously Dim: The Poetry of Robert Penn Warren," *Fresco,* I (1960), 43-55.

*Edmonds, Irene. "Robert Penn Warren and the 'Tragic Mulatto,' " *New York Review,* I (Spring, 1958), 19-22.

*Ellison, Ralph, and Walter, Eugene. "The Art of Fiction XVIII: Robert Penn Warren," *Paris Review,* IV (Spring-Summer, 1957), 112-140. Reprinted as follows:

"Robert Penn Warren," *Writers at Work: The Paris Review Interviews*. Edited by Malcolm Cowley. New York: The Viking Press, 1958, pp. 183-207;
"The Art of Fiction XVIII: Robert Penn Warren," *Robert Penn Warren: A Collection of Critical Essays*. Edited by John Lewis Longley, Jr. New York: New York University Press, 1965, pp. 18-45.

———, and ———. "Robert Penn Warren." See "The Art of Fiction XVIII: Robert Penn Warren."

*Engelborghs, M. "Drie Romans van Robert Penn Warren," *Kultuurleven*, XXVII (July, 1960), 446-454.

England, Kenneth. "They Came Home Again: Fugitives' Return," *Georgia Review*, XIV (Spring, 1960), 80-89.

"Fables for Our Time," [London] *Times Literary Supplement*, November 27, 1959, p. 692.

Fergusson, Francis. "Three Novels," *Perspectives USA*, No. 6 (Winter, 1954), 30-44.

Fiedler, Leslie A. "On Two Frontiers," *Partisan Review*, XVII September-October, 1950), 739-743.

———. "Romance in the Operatic Manner," *New Republic*, CXXXIII (September 26, 1955), 28-30.

Fitts, Dudley. "Of Tragic Stature," *Poetry*, LXV (November, 1944), 94-101.

Fitzell, Lincoln. "The Sword and the Dragon," *South Atlantic Quarterly*, L (April, 1951), 230-231.

"Five Music Men of Words," *Newsweek*, LI (March 17, 1958), 110.
Biographical sketch of Warren.

Fletcher, John Gould. "The Modern Southern Poets," *Westminster Magazine*, XXIII (Winter, 1935), 229-251.

Flint, F. Cudworth. "Five Poets," *Southern Review*, I (Winter, 1936) 650-674.

———. "Mr. Warren and the Reviewers," *Sewanee Review*, LXIV (Autumn, 1956), 632-645. Reprinted in *Robert Penn Warren: A Collection of Critical Essays*. Edited by John Lewis Longley, Jr. New York: New York University Press, 1965, pp. 125-139.

———. "Robert Penn Warren," *American Oxonian*, XXXIV (April, 1947), 65-79.

Fogle, Richard Harter. "A Recent Attack upon Romanticism," *College English*, IX (April, 1948), 356-361.

Ford, Newell F. "Kenneth Burke and Robert Penn Warren: Criticism by Obsessive Metaphor," *Journal of English and Germanic Philology*, LIII (April, 1954), 172-177.

Forgotson, E. S. "The Poetic Method of Robert Penn Warren," *American Prefaces*, VI (Winter, 1941), 130-146.

*Fortin, Marilyn B. "Jack Burden's Search for Identity in *All the King's Men*," *Kansas Magazine*, No. 4 (1963), 33-37.

Frank, Joseph. "Romanticism and Reality in Robert Penn Warren," *Hudson Review*, IV (Summer, 1951), 248-258. Reprinted in *The Widening Gyre: Crisis and Mastery in Modern Literature*. By Joseph Frank. New Brunswick, New Jersey: Rutgers University Press, 1963, pp. 179-202.

Frank, William. "Warren's Achievement," *College English*, XIX (May, 1958), 365-366.

Frohock, W. M. "Mr. Warren's Albatross," *Southwest Review*, XXXVI (Winter, 1951), 48-59. Reprinted in *The Novel of Violence in America*. By W. M. Frohock. Second edition, revised and enlarged. Dallas: Southern Methodist University Press, 1957, pp. 86-105.

Frost, William. "Warren's *Pursuit*," *Explicator*, XI (February, 1953), Item 22. Reprinted in *The Explicator Cyclopedia*. Edited by Charles Child Walcutt and J. Edwin Whitesell. Chicago: Quadrangle Books, 1966, Vol. I, pp. 338-339.

*Fuchs, Carolyn. "Words, Action, and the Modern Novel," *Kerygma*, IV (Winter, 1964), 3-11.

G., R. "The Author," *Saturday Review of Literature*, XXXIII (June 24, 1950), 11.
Biographical sketch.

Gabrieli, Vittorio. "Romanticismo E Visione Tragica Nel Romanzo Di R. P. Warren," *Lo Spettatore Italiano*, IV (Gennaio, 1951), 12-14; Febbraio, 1951), 38-41. (In two installments).

Garrett, George Palmer. "The Function of the Pasiphae Myth in *Brother to Dragons*," *Modern Language Notes*, LXXIV (April, 1959), 311-313.

Gerard, Albert. "Robert Penn Warren, romancier de la responsabilité," *Revue générale belge*, Octobre, 1960, pp. 27-39.

Gerhard, George. "*All the King's Men:* A Symposium," *Folio*, XV (May, 1950), 4-11.

Gibbs, Wolcott. "The Theatre: Midseason Miscellany," *New Yorker*, XXIII (January 24, 1948), 42-43.

Girault, Norton R. "The Narrator's Mind as Symbol: An Analysis of *All the King's Men*," *Accent*, VII (Summer, 1947), 220-234. Reprinted in *Critiques and Essays on Modern Fiction, 1920-1951*. Edited by John W. Aldridge. New York: The Ronald Press Company, 1952, pp. 200-216.

*Glazier, Lyle. "Reconstructed Platonism: Robert Penn Warren's *The Cave*," *Litera*, VII (1960), 16-26.

*Godfrey, L. "Robert Penn Warren's Vision of Time," *Osmania Journal of English Studies* (Osmania University, Hyderabad), No. 2, pp. 29-36.

Gordon, Clifford M. "Warren's *Original Sin: A Short Story*," *Explicator*, IX (December, 1950), Item 21. Reprinted in *The Explicator Cyclopedia*. Edited by Charles Child Walcutt and J. Edwin Whitesell. Chicago: Quadrangle Books, 1966, Vol. I, pp. 337-338.

Grantham, Dewey W., Jr. "Interpreters of the Modern South," *South Atlantic Quarterly*, LXIII (Autumn, 1964), 521-529.

Gregory, Horace. "Of Vitality, Regionalism, and Satire in Recent American Poetry," *Sewanee Review*, LII (Autumn, 1944), 575-578.

Gross, Harvey. "History as Metaphysical Pathos: Modern Literature and the Idea of History," *Denver Quarterly*, I (Autumn, 1966), 1-22.

Gross, Seymour L. "The Achievement of Robert Penn Warren," *College English*, XIX (May, 1958), 361-365.

———. "Conrad and *All the King's Men*," *Twentieth Century Literature*, III (April, 1957), 27-32.

———. "Laurence Sterne and Eliot's 'Prufrock': An Object Lesson in Explication," *College English*, XIX (November, 1957), 72-73.

———. "Robert Penn Warren," *Critic*, XVIII (October-November, 1959), 11-13, 80-82.

Guthrie, A. B., Jr. "Virtue Plundered in Kentucky," *Saturday Review of Literature*, XXXIII (June 24, 1950), 11-12.

Hardwick, Elizabeth. "Poor Little Rich Girls," *Partisan Review*, XII (Summer, 1945), 420-422.

A study of Sue Murdock in Warren's *At Heaven's Gate* and Hopestill Mather in Jean Stafford's *Boston Adventure*.

Hardy, John Edward. "Robert Penn Warren's Double-Hero," *Virginia Quarterly Review*, XXXVI (Autumn, 1960), 583-597.

Hartsock, Ernest. "Roses in the Desert: A View of Contemporary Southern Verse," *Sewanee Review*, XXXVII (July, 1929), 328-335.

*Hashiguchi, Yasuo. "A Critical Analysis of Robert Penn Warren's 'Blackberry Winter,'" *Kyusha American Literature* (Fukuoka, Japan), No. 2 (May, 1959), 23-27.

*———. "Robert Penn Warren as a Short Story Writer," *Kyusha American Literature* (Fukuoka, Japan), No. 1 (June, 1958), 19-25.

Havard, William C. "The Burden of the Literary Mind: Some Meditations on Robert Penn Warren as Historian," *South Atlantic Quarterly*, LXII (Autumn, 1963), 516-531. Reprinted in *Robert Penn Warren: A Collection of Critical Essays*. Edited by John Lewis Longley, Jr. New York: New York University Press, 1965, pp. 178-194.

*Hayashi, Nobunyuki. "On the Novels of Robert Penn Warren," *Jinbun Gakuho* (Tokyo Metropolitan University), No. 28 (March, 1962), 3-24.

Heilman, Robert B. "Melpomene as Wallflower; or, The Reading of Tragedy," *Sewanee Review*, LV (January-March, 1947), 154-166. Reprinted in *Robert Penn Warren: A Collection of Critical Essays*. Edited by John Lewis Longley, Jr. New York: New York University Press, 1965, pp. 82-95.

———. "The Southern Temper," *Hopkins Review*, VI (Fall, 1952), 5-15.

———. "Tangled Web," *Sewanee Review*, LIX (Winter, 1951), 107-119. Reprinted in *Robert Penn Warren: A Collection of Critical Essays*. Edited by John Lewis Longley, Jr. New York: New York University Press, 1965, pp. 96-109.

Hendry, Irene. "The Regional Novel: the Example of Robert Penn Warren," *Sewanee Review*, LIII (January-March, 1945), 84-102.

Herschberger, Ruth. "Poised between the two alarms . . . ," *Accent*, IV (Summer, 1944), 240-246. Reprinted in *Accent Anthology*. Edited by Kerker Quinn and Charles Shattuck. New York: Harcourt, Brace and Company, 1946, pp. 610-618.

*Heseltine, Harry P. "The Deep, Twisting Strain of Life: The Novels of Robert Penn Warren," *Melbourne Critical Review* (University of Melbourne), No. 5 (1962), 76-89.

Hicks, John. "Exploration of Value: Warren's Criticism," *South Atlantic Quarterly*, LXII (Autumn, 1963), 508-515.

Holland, Robert B. "The Agrarian Manifesto: A Generation Later," *Mississippi Quarterly*, X (Spring, 1957), 73-78.

Holman, C. Hugh. "Literature and Culture: The *Fugitive*-Agrarians," *Social Forces*, XXXVII (October, 1958), 15-19.

Holmes, Theodore. "The Literary Mode," *Carleton Miscellany*, IV (Winter, 1963), 124-128.

Hudson, Richard B. "*All the King's Men:* A Symposium," *Folio*, XV (May, 1950), 11-13.

Humboldt, Charles. "The Lost Cause of Robert Penn Warren," *Masses and Mainstream*, I (July, 1948), 8-20.

Hutchens, John K. "On an Author," *New York Herald Tribune Book Review*, XXVI (July 2, 1950), 2.

Hynes, Sam. "Robert Penn Warren: The Symbolic Journey," *University of Kansas City Review*, XVII (Summer, 1951), 279-285.

Irish, Marion D. "Proposed Roads to the New South, 1941: Chapel Hill Planners vs. Nashville Agrarians," *Sewanee Review*, XLIX (January-March, 1941), 1-27.

Jacobs, Robert D. "Faulkner's Tragedy of Isolation," *Hopkins Review*, VI (Spring-Summer, 1953), 162-183.

______. "Poe and the Agrarian Critics," *Hopkins Review*, V (Spring, 1952), 43-54.

Jones, Madison. "The Novels of Robert Penn Warren," *South Atlantic Quarterly*, LXII (Autumn, 1963), 488-498.

Justus, James H. "The Mariner and Robert Penn Warren," *Texas Studies in Literature and Language*, VIII (Spring, 1966), 117-128.

______. "The Uses of Gesture in Warren's *The Cave*," *Modern Language Quarterly*, XXVI (September, 1965), 448-461.

______. "Warren's *World Enough and Time* and Beauchamp's *Confession*," *American Literature*, XXXIII (January, 1962), 500-511.

Kalb, Bernard. "The Author," *Saturday Review*, XXXVIII (August 20, 1955), 9.

Kaplan, Charles. "Jack Burden: Modern Ishmael," *College English*, XXII (October, 1960), 19-24.

Kazin, Alfred. " 'A City of the Soul,' " *Reporter*, XXIV (June 8, 1961), 40-44. Reprinted as "The Southern 'City of the Soul' " in *Contemporaries*. By Alfred Kazin. Boston: Little, Brown and Company, 1962, pp. 178-183.

———. "The Seriousness of Robert Penn Warren," *Partisan Review*, XXVI (Spring, 1959), 312-316.

———. "The Southern 'City of the Soul.' " See " 'A City of the Soul.' "

Kelvin, Norman. "The Failure of Robert Penn Warren," *College English*, XVIII (April, 1957), 355-364.

Kennedy, William. " 'Saying the Unsayable': How a Poet Works," *National Observer*, VI (February 6, 1967), 31.
A feature on Warren's visit to Union College, Schenectady, New York. Includes several statements by Warren.

*Kerr, Dell. "An Exercise on Robert Penn Warren's *All the King's Men*," *Exercise Exchange*, V (October, 1957), 8-9.

Kerr, Elizabeth M. "Polarity of Themes in *All the King's Men*," *Modern Fiction Studies*, VI (Spring, 1960), 25-46.

King, Roma A., Jr. "Time and Structure in the Early Novels of Robert Penn Warren," *South Atlantic Quarterly*, LVI (Autumn, 1957), 486-493.

Knickerbocker, William S. "The Fugitives of Nashville," *Sewanee Review*, XXXVI (April, 1928), 211-224.

*Lemaire, Marcel. "Fiction in U. S. A. From the South . . . ," *Revue des Langues Vivantes*, XXVII (1961), 244-253.

*Létargeez, J. "Robert Penn Warren's Views of History," *Revue des Langues Vivantes*, XXII (1956), 533-543.

"Letters to the Editor," *New York Times Book Review*, January 15, 1956, p. 32.

Prints excerpts from letters provoked by Warren's essay "A Lesson Read in American Books."

"Letters to the Editor," *New York Times Book Review*, October 7, 1956, p. 44.

Includes letters commenting on Warren's *Segregation: The Inner Conflict in the South.*

Link, Franz H. "Das Verhältnis der Dichtung zur Wirklichkeit bei Allen Tate und anderen *new critics*," *Deutsche Vierteljahrsschrift für Literaturwissenschaft und Geistesgeschichte*, XXXIV (December, 1960), 554-580.

———. "Uber das Geschichtsbewusstsein einiger amerikanischer Dichter des 20. Jahrhunderts: Hart Cranes *The Bridge*, Stephen Vincent Benéts *Western Star* und Robert Penn Warrens *Brother to Dragons*," *Jahrbuch für Amerikastudien*, IV (1959), 143-160.

*Lombardo, Agostino. "Poesia di R. P. Warren," *Criterio*, II (1958), 33-41.

Long, Louise. "*Night Rider*," *Southwest Review*, XXIV (July, 1939), 498-500.

Longley, John Lewis, Jr. "'At Heaven's Gate': The Major Themes," *Modern Fiction Studies*, VI (Spring, 1960), 13-24. Reprinted in revised form as "Self-Knowledge, The Pearl of Pus, and the Seventh Circle: The Major Themes in *At Heaven's Gate*" in *Robert Penn Warren: A Collection of Critical Essays.* Edited by John Lewis Longley, Jr. New York: New York University Press, 1965, p. 60-74.

*———. "Robert Penn Warren: American Man of Letters," *Arts and Sciences* (New York University), Spring, 1965, pp. 16-22.

———. "Robert Penn Warren: The Deeper Rub," *Southern Review*, n.s. I (Autumn, 1965), 968-980.

———. "Self-Knowledge, The Pearl of Pus, and the Seventh Circle: The Major Themes in *At Heaven's Gate*." See "'At Heaven's Gate': The Major Themes."

Lowell, Robert. "Prose Genius in Verse," *Kenyon Review,* XV (Autumn, 1953), 619-625.

Lytle, Andrew. "At Heaven's Gate," *Sewanee Review,* LI (October-December, 1943), 599-602.

McDowell, Frederick P. W. "Psychology and Theme in *Brother to Dragons,*" *Publications of the Modern Language Association,* LXX (September, 1955), 565-586. Reprinted in *Robert Penn Warren: A Collection of Critical Essays.* Edited by John Lewis Longley, Jr. New York: New York University Press, 1965, pp. 197-222.

———. "Robert Penn Warren's Criticism," *Accent,* XV (Summer, 1955), 173-196.
Includes a selective bibliography of Robert Penn Warren's critical writings (pp. 195-196).

———. "The Romantic Tragedy of Self in *World Enough and Time,*" *Critique: Studies in Modern Fiction,* I (Summer, 1957), 34-48. Reprinted in *Robert Penn Warren: A Collection of Critical Essays.* Edited by John Lewis Longley, Jr. New York: New York University Press, 1965, pp. 110-124.

*McElderry, B. R., Jr. "Robert Penn Warren and Whitman," *Walt Whitman Review,* VIII (December, 1962), 91.

McGill, Ralph. "Red Warren Soaked Up the South's Raw Agony," *Nashville Tennessean,* LXI (February 28, 1967), 7.
Biographical feature on Warren.

Magmer, James, S. J. "Robert Penn Warren's Quest for an Angel," *Catholic World,* CLXXXIII (June, 1956), 178-183.

Marion, Denis. "Robert Penn Warren," *Nouvelle Nouvelle Revue Française,* I (April, 1953), 725-728.

Marshall, Margaret. "Notes by the Way," *Nation,* CLXVI (February 21, 1948), 216.
On "The Circus in the Attic."

Martin, Terence. "*Band of Angels*: The Definition of Self-Definition," *Folio,* XXI (Winter, 1956), 31-37.

Matthiessen, F. O. "American Poetry, 1920-40," *Sewanee Review*, LV (January-March, 1947), 24-55.

———. "American Poetry Now," *Kenyon Review*, VI (Autumn, 1944), 683-696.

Mizener, Arthur. "Amphibium in Old Kentucky," *Kenyon Review*, XII (Autumn, 1950), 697-701.

———. "Robert Penn Warren: *All the King's Men*," *Southern Review*, n.s. III (Autumn, 1967), 874-894.

———. "The Uncorrupted Consciousness," *Sewanee Review*, LXXII (Autumn, 1964), 690-698.

Modern Fiction Studies, VI (Spring, 1960). (The Robert Penn Warren Special Number.)

Contains seven essays (listed separately in this bibliography) and a checklist of selected criticism of Warren. Checklist includes the following sections: "General Studies," "Studies Primarily on the Poetry," and "Studies of Individual Works of Fiction."

Mohrt, Michel. "Robert Penn Warren and the Myth of the Outlaw," *Yale French Studies*, No. 10, pp. 70-84. First published as the introduction for Pierre Singer's French translation of *All the King's Men*. Also published as "Robert Penn Warren Ou Le Mythe Du Hors-La-Loi" in *Le Nouveau Roman Américain*. By Michel Mohrt. Paris: Gallimard, 1955, pp. 207-223.

———. "Robert Penn Warren Ou Le Mythe Du Hors-La-Loi." See "Robert Penn Warren and the Myth of the Outlaw."

Montague, John. "American Pegasus," *Studies*, XLVIII (Summer, 1959), 183-191.

Montgomery, Marion. "Bells for John Stewart's Burden: A Sermon upon the Desirable Death of the 'New Provincialism' Here Typified," *Georgia Review*, XX (Summer, 1966), 145-181.

Montgomery, Paul L. "Dinner Salutes Pulitzer Prizes," *New York Times*, May 11, 1966, p. 33.

Gives a resumé of Warren's remarks—concerning the present status of the novel—made at the fiftieth anniversary celebration of the Pulitzer prizes.

*Moore, L. Hugh. "Robert Penn Warren, William Styron, and the Use of the Greek Myth," *Critique: Studies in Modern Fiction,* VIII (Winter, 1965-1966), 75-87.

Morrissey, Ralph. "The Fugitives Return," *New York Times Book Review,* May 20, 1956, p. 27.
A report on the Fugitives' reunion at Vanderbilt; includes a quotation by Warren on the "exhaustive documentation being compiled on [the Fugitives]." Also contains a brief history of the group.

Muller, Herbert J. "Violence upon the Roads," *Kenyon Review,* I (Summer, 1939), 323-324.

Munro, David A. "A Case?—for 'Semi-Fiction,'" *Trace,* No. 48 (Spring, 1963), 17-19.

Munson, Gorham B. [Letter], *New Republic,* LV (June 27, 1928), 149.
A letter in which an incidental comment on Warren's review of Munson occurs.

Nathan, Monique. ["Les Fous du Roi de Robert Penn Warren"], *Critique* (Paris), VII (May, 1951), 467-470.

Nemerov, Howard. "The Phoenix in the World," *Furioso,* III (Spring, 1948), 36-46.

New York Times News Service. "Warren Poetry Cited," *Nashville Tennessean,* LXI (February 6, 1967), 5.
Announces Warren's winning the Bollingen Prize in poetry.

O'Connor, William Van. "The Burden of Innocence," *Sewanee Review,* LXII (Winter, 1954), 143-150.

———. "The Influence of the Metaphysicals on Modern Poetry," *College English,* IX (January, 1948), 180-187.

———. "Robert Penn Warren's Short Fiction," *Western Review,* XII (Summer, 1948), 251-253.

*Phillips, William L. "Study Guides: Robert Penn Warren's *All the King's Men*," *Exercise Exchange*, I, No. 4, pp. 6-7.

"Poet and Arguer: Robert Penn Warren," *New York Times*, February 6, 1967, p. 32.
Biographical sketch of Warren on the occasion of his winning the Bollingen Prize in Poetry.

Pressly, Thomas J. "Agrarianism: An Autopsy," *Sewanee Review*, XLIX (April-June, 1941), 145-163.

"Prized Poet," *Newsweek*, LXIX (February 20, 1967), 96.
Announces Warren's winning the $5,000 Bollingen Prize for Poetry, given for *Selected Poems: New and Old, 1923-1966.*

"Pulitzer, 1958," *New York Times*, May 6, 1958, p. 34.
An editorial mentioning Warren's winning a Pulitzer Prize for *Promises: Poems 1954-1956.*

Raben, Joseph. "*All the King's Men*: A Symposium," *Folio*, XV (May, 1950), 14-18.

Ransom, John Crowe. "*All the King's Men*: A Symposium," *Folio*, XV (May, 1950), 2-3.

———. "Hearts and Heads," *American Review*, II (March, 1934), 554-571.

———. "The Inklings of 'Original Sin,'" *Saturday Review of Literature*, XXVII (May 20, 1944), 10-11.

Rathbun, John W. "Philosophy, *World Enough and Time*, and the Art of the Novel," *Modern Fiction Studies*, VI (Spring, 1960), 47-54.

Ray, Robert J., and Ray, Ann. "Time in *All the King's Men*: A Stylistic Analysis," *Texas Studies in Literature and Language*, V (Autumn, 1963), 452-457.

Reddick, L. D. "Whose Ordeal?" *New Republic*, CXXXV (September 24, 1956), 9-10.

Renguette, Dale T. "The Gray Pessimism of Robert Penn Warren," *Fresco*, I, No. 1 (1960), 34-42.

Rosenthal, M. L. "Robert Penn Warren's Poetry," *South Atlantic Quarterly*, LXII (Autumn, 1963), 499-507.

Rouse, H. Blair. "Time and Place in Southern Fiction," *Hopkins Review*, VI (Fall, 1952), 37-61.

Rubin, Louis D., Jr. "All the King's Meanings," *Georgia Review*, VIII (Winter, 1954), 422-434.

———. "The Concept of Nature in Modern Southern Poetry," *American Quarterly*, IX (Spring, 1957), 63-71.

———. "The Eye of Time: Religious Themes in Robert Penn Warren's Poetry," *Diliman Review* [Philippines], III (July, 1955), 215-237.

———. "The South and the Faraway Country," *Virginia Quarterly Review*, XXXVIII (Summer, 1962), 444-459.

———. "The Southern Muse: Two Poetry Societies," *American Quarterly*, XIII (Fall, 1961), 365-375.

———. " 'Theories of Human Nature': Kazin or Warren?" *Sewanee Review*, LXIX (Summer, 1961), 500-506.

Runnquist, Åke. "Pärlan i ostronet: Några drag i Robert Penn Warrens romaner," *Bonniers Litterära Magasin* (Stockholm), XVI (November, 1947), 725-732.

Ruoff, James. "Humpty Dumpty and *All the King's Men*: A Note on Robert Penn Warren's Teleology," *Twentieth Century Literature*, III (October, 1957), 128-134.

———. "Robert Penn Warren's Pursuit of Justice: From Briar Patch to Cosmos," *Research Studies of the State College of Washington*, XXVII (March, 1959), 19-38.

Ryan, Alvan S. "Robert Penn Warren's *Night Rider*: The Nihilism of the Isolated Temperament," *Modern Fiction Studies*, VII (Winter, 1961-1962), 338-346. Reprinted in *Robert Penn Warren: A Collection of Critical Essays*. Edited by John Lewis Longley, Jr. New York: New York University Press, 1965, pp. 49-59.

Sale, Roger. "Having It Both Ways in *All the King's Men*," *Hudson Review*, XIV (Spring, 1961), 68-76.

Samuels, Charles Thomas. "In the Wilderness," *Critique: Studies in Modern Fiction*, V (Fall, 1962), 46-57.

Saporta, Marc. "Robert Penn Warren," *Informations & Documents*, No. 187, pp. 6-7.

Satterwhite, Joseph N. "Robert Penn Warren and Emily Dickinson," *Modern Language Notes*, LXXI (May, 1956), 347-349.

Saturday Evening Post, CCXXXVII (April 4, 1964), 41. Biographical sketch of Warren.

Schiller, Andrew. "The World Out of Square," *Western Review*, XV (Spring, 1951), 234-237.

Schwartz, Elias. "Ransom's 'Bells for John Whiteside's Daughter,' " *English Language Notes*, I (June, 1964), 284-285.

Scott, James B. "The Theme of Betrayal in Robert Penn Warren's Stories," *Thoth*, V (Spring, 1964), 74-84.

Sherbo, Arthur. "Sherwood Anderson's *I Want to Know Why* and Messrs. Brooks and Warren," *College English*, XV (March, 1954), 350-351.

Sillars, Malcolm O. "Warren's *All the King's Men*: A Study in Populism," *American Quarterly*, IX (Fall, 1957), 345-353.

"Sketches of the Pulitzer Prize Winners for 1958 in Letters, Music and Journalism," *New York Times*, May 6, 1958, p. 38.
Biographical sketch of Warren.

[Skillin, Edward, Jr.] "Mighty Like Despair," *Commonweal*, XXXVIII (August 6, 1943), 398.

Southard, W. P. "The Religious Poetry of Robert Penn Warren," *Kenyon Review*, VII (Autumn, 1945), 653-676.

"The Southern Review," *Vanderbilt Alumnus*, XXVI (November, 1940), 8-9.

Stallknecht, Newton P. "*All the King's Men*: A Symposium," *Folio*, XV (May, 1950), 18-22.

Stallman, Robert Wooster. "Robert Penn Warren: A Checklist of His Critical Writings," *University of Kansas City Review*, XIV (Autumn, 1947), 78-83.

"Checklist is limited to [Warren's] writings on poetry and criticism (it excludes writings on fiction), and it presents criticisms on the author's poetic and critical work." Contains three sections:

I. "His Books and Essays";
II. "His Reviews";
III. "Criticism on Warren."

Starke, Aubrey. "The Agrarians Deny a Leader," *American Review*, II (March, 1934), 534-553.

Stewart, James T. "Two Uses of Maupassant by R. P. Warren," *Modern Language Notes*, LXX (April, 1955), 279-280.

Stewart, John L. "The Achievement of Robert Penn Warren," *South Atlantic Quarterly*, XLVII (October, 1948), 562-579.

———. "Robert Penn Warren and the Knot of History," *Journal of English Literary History*, XXVI (March, 1959), 102-136.

Stewart, Randall. "Dreiser and the Naturalistic Heresy," *Virginia Quarterly Review*, XXXIV (Winter, 1958), 100-116.

Concludes that Warren and other ". . . great Southern fiction writers of our time have brought our literature back [from Naturalism] to the tradition of Hawthorne and Melville, of Milton and Shakespeare."

Strandberg, Victor H. "Theme and Metaphor in *Brother to Dragons*," *Publications of the Modern Language Association*, LXXIX (September, 1964), 498-508. Reprinted as most of the chapter entitled "*Brother to Dragons*: 'Warren's Best Book' " in *A Colder Fire: The Poetry of Robert Penn Warren*. By Victor H. Strandberg. Lexington: University of Kentucky Press, 1965, pp. 139-168.

Strugnell, John R. "Robert Penn Warren and the Uses of the Past," *Review of English Literature*, IV (October, 1963), 93-102.

Sutherland, Ronald. "Structural Linguistics and English Prosody," *College English,* XX (October, 1958), 12-17.

"A Symposium: The Agrarians Today," *Shenandoah,* III (Summer, 1952), 14-33.

Tate, Allen. "*The Fugitive* 1922-1925: A Personal Recollection Twenty Years After," *Princeton University Library Chronicle,* III (April, 1942), 75-84.

Thale, Jerome. "The Narrator as Hero," *Twentieth Century Literature,* III (July, 1957), 69-73.

"[Three] Members Added by Arts Academy," *New York Times,* December 5, 1959, p. 8.

Announces Warren's election to the American Academy of Arts and Letters.

Time, XXXIII (March 27, 1939), 73.

Biographical sketch of Warren.

Tyler, Parker. "An American Theater Motif: The Psychodrama," *American Quarterly,* XV (Summer, 1963), 140-151.

———. "Novel into Film: *All the King's Men,*" *Kenyon Review,* XII (Spring, 1950), 369-376. Reprinted in *The Kenyon Critics: Studies in Modern Literature.* Edited by John Crowe Ransom. Cleveland and New York: World Publishing Company, 1951, pp. 225-232.

*Vidal, Gore. "Book Report," *Zero,* II (Spring, 1956), 95-98.

Virtanen, Reino. "Camus' *Le Malentendu* and Some Analogues," *Comparative Literature,* X (Summer, 1958), 232-240.

Walcutt, Charles Child. "The Regional Novel and Its Future," *Arizona Quarterly,* I (Summer, 1945), 17-27.

Wasserstrom, William. "Robert Penn Warren: From Paleface to Redskin," *Prairie Schooner,* XXXI (Winter, 1957-1958), 323-333.

———. "Warren's New Poems," *Prairie Schooner,* XXXII (Spring, 1958), 67-69.

Watkins, Floyd C. "Billie Potts at the Fall of Time," *Mississippi Quarterly*, XI (Winter, 1958), 19-28.

———. "Thomas Wolfe and the Nashville Agrarians," *Georgia Review*, VII (Winter, 1953), 410-423.

Weathers, Winston. " 'Blackberry Winter' and the Use of Archetypes," *Studies in Short Fiction*, I (Fall, 1963), 45-51.

Weisbuch, Ted N. "Jack Burden: Call Me Carraway," *College English*, XXII (February, 1961), 361.

West, Ray B., Jr. "Truth, Beauty, and American Criticism," *University of Kansas City Review*, XIV (Winter, 1947), 137-148.

White, Robert. "Robert Penn Warren and the Myth of the Garden," *Faulkner Studies*, III (Winter, 1954), 59-67.

Whittemore, Reed. "A Few Ways of Pulling Apart a Poem," *New Republic*, CXXXVII (December 9, 1957), 15-19.

"Who's Who in the Library of Congress: Mr. Robert Penn Warren," [U. S. Library of Congress] *Information Bulletin*, September, 1944, pp. 4, 6.

Widmer, Kingsley. "The Father-Killers of R. P. Warren," *Paunch*, No. 22 (January, 1965), 57-64.

Wood, James P. "Mr. Warren's 'Modern Realism,' " *Saturday Review of Literature*, XXIX (August 17, 1946), 11.

"Works in Progress 1963," *Esquire*, LX (July, 1963), 50-51, 55-56, 105. [An excerpt from Warren's *Flood* appears on pp. 55-56.]

Wright, James. "The Stiff Smile of Mr. Warren," *Kenyon Review*, XX (Autumn, 1958), 645-655.

Yanagi, Kiichirō. "*Night Rider* and Robert Penn Warren's Ideas," *Bulletin of the University of Osaka Prefecture*, Series C, IX (1961), 57-72.

Z[abel], M. D. "Problems of Knowledge," *Poetry*, XLVIII (April, 1936), 37-41.

UNPUBLISHED THESES AND DISSERTATIONS

Altgelt, Frederick. "Robert Penn Warren. A Study of Symbolism in *Night Rider* and *World Enough and Time*." Unpublished Master's thesis, Department of English, Vanderbilt University, 1954.

Auerbach, M. Morton. "Conservatism and its Contemporary American Advocates." Unpublished Ph.D. dissertation, Columbia University, 1958. Abstracted in *Dissertation Abstracts*, XIX (1958), 857.

Bennett, John. "The Iron Beach: A Study of the Poetry of Robert Penn Warren." Unpublished Master's thesis, Department of English, Vanderbilt University, 1948.

Borchers, Nancy Norris. "Robert Penn Warren's Novels: The Differences within the Framework of the Similarities." Unpublished Master's thesis, Department of English, Vanderbilt University, 1958.

Bowen, Frances Jean. "*The New Orleans Double Dealer*: 1921-May 1926, A Critical History." Unpublished Ph.D. dissertation, Vanderbilt University, 1954. Abstracted in *Dissertation Abstracts*, XIV (1954), 2063.

Includes a bio-critical sketch of Warren, as well as copies of his poems appearing in *The Double Dealer*, on pp. 395-398.

Bradbury, John Mason. "The Fugitive Critics: A Critical History." Unpublished Ph.D. dissertation, State University of Iowa, 1948.

Revised and printed as *The Fugitives: A Critical Account.*

Casey, James R. "The Short Stories in the *Southern Review* (1935-42)." Unpublished Master's thesis, Department of English, Vanderbilt University, 1949.

Casper, Leonard Ralph. "The Lost Sense of Community and the Role of the Artist in Robert Penn Warren." Unpublished Ph.D. dissertation, University of Wisconsin, 1953. Abstracted in *Summaries of Doctoral Dissertations: University of Wisconsin*, XIV (1954), 426-428.

Clark, Marden J. "Symbolic Structure in the Novels of Robert Penn Warren." Unpublished Ph.D. dissertation, University of Washington, 1957. Abstracted in *Dissertation Abstracts,* XVIII (1958), 229-230.

*Coleman, Thomas Emmett, Jr. "Form as Function in the Novels of Robert Penn Warren." Unpublished Master's thesis, University of Louisville, 1950.

Cook, Martha Emily. "From Fact to Fiction: A Study of Robert Penn Warren's *World Enough and Time.*" Unpublished Master's thesis, Department of English, Vanderbilt University, 1967.

Godsey, Edwin S. "The Development of Tragedy in Four Novels by Robert Penn Warren." Unpublished Master's thesis, Department of English, Vanderbilt University, 1954.

Harrison, Jane. "The Fiction of Robert Penn Warren: A Study in Technique." Unpublished Master's thesis, Department of English, Vanderbilt University, 1947.

*Hynes, Sam. "The Poet as Dramatist: Robert Penn Warren and Some Predecessors." Unpublished Master's thesis, Columbia University, 1948.

Justus, James Huff. "The Concept of Gesture in the Novels of Robert Penn Warren." Unpublished Ph.D. dissertation, University of Washington, 1961. Abstracted in *Dissertation Abstracts,* XXII (1962), 3201.

Lane, Calvin Warren. "Narrative Art and History in Robert Penn Warren's *World Enough and Time.*" Unpublished Ph.D. dissertation, University of Michigan, 1956. Abstracted in *Dissertation Abstracts,* XVII (1957), 1340.

Linenthal, Mark, Jr. "Robert Penn Warren and the Southern Agrarians." Unpublished Ph.D. dissertation, Stanford University, 1957. Abstracted in *Dissertation Abstracts,* XVII (1957), 2611-2612.

Moore, Littleton Hugh, Jr. "Robert Penn Warren and History: 'The Big Myth We Live.'" Unpublished Ph.D. dissertation,

Emory University, 1964. Abstracted in *Dissertation Abstracts*, XXV (1965), 5283-5284.

Poenicke, Klaus. "Schöpferische Dialektik: Kunswerk und kritische Theorie bei Robert Penn Warren." Unpublished Ph.D. dissertation, Freie Universität (Berlin), 1957.

Prater, Neal B. "Point of View in the Novels of Robert Penn Warren." Unpublished Master's thesis, Department of English, Vanderbilt University, 1959.

Rock, Virginia Jeanne. "The Making and Meaning of *I'll Take My Stand*: A Study of Utopian-Conservatism." Unpublished Ph.D. dissertation, University of Minnesota, [1960-1961?].

Samuels, Charles Thomas. "Robert Penn Warren: The End and the Beginning." Unpublished Ph.D. dissertation, University of California, Berkeley, [1961-1962?].

Shepherd, Allen Glass, III. "A Critical Study of the Fiction of Robert Penn Warren." Unpublished Ph.D. dissertation, University of Pennsylvania, 1965. Abstracted in *Dissertation Abstracts*, XXVI (1966), 7325-7326.

Stewart, John Lincoln. "The Fugitive-Agrarian Writers: A History and a Criticism." Unpublished Ph.D. dissertation, Ohio State University, Summer Quarter, 1947-48. Revised and printed as *The Burden of Time: The Fugitives and Agrarians*. Dissertation abstracted in *Abstracts of Dissertations*, The Ohio State University. No. 55. Columbus: Ohio State University, 1949, pp. 295-302.

Stone, Edith Opal. "Democratic Values in Modern Narrative Poems." Unpublished Ph.D. dissertation, University of Michigan, 1960. Abstracted in *Dissertation Abstracts*, XXI (1960), 345.

Strandberg, Victor Hugo. "Robert Penn Warren as Poet: A Close Analysis of *Selected Poems, Brother to Dragons, Promises* and *You, Emperors, and Others*." Unpublished Ph.D. dissertation, Brown University, 1962. Abstracted in *Dissertation Abstracts*, XXIII (1962), 2141-2142.

Welker, Robert Louis. "Evelyn Scott: A Literary Biography." Unpublished Ph.D. dissertation, Vanderbilt University, 1958. Abstracted in *Dissertation Abstracts*, XIX (1958), 1080-1081.

Examines the regional influence on ". . . the aesthetics and underlying philosophical tenets . . ." of Warren, Caroline Gordon, and other contemporary writers from the same region as Evelyn Scott.

———. "The Underlying Philosophy of Robert Penn Warren: A Study in the Poetic Attitude." Unpublished Master's thesis, Department of English, Vanderbilt University, 1952.

Whittington, Curtis C., Jr. "Dialectic Humanism and the Theme of Robert Penn Warren." Unpublished Master's thesis, Department of English, Vanderbilt University, 1955.